Miracles with Mommy Linda is dedicated to Pastor Maxeau Antoine

As I am writing this dedication, Pastor Maxeau, his wife, and youngest daughter are in- hiding in the country of Haiti and unable to return to their home. They have chosen to split up in three different locations after learning that the head of the strongest gang in Haiti and some of the leader's members were found outside of Maxeau's home attempting to open the gate and breach the security wall. Maxeau's neighbors contacted him and told him not to return home. As of this moment, we are waiting to see if the police (which are basically non-existent in Haiti) will move in and take charge. If not, the area where Maxeau currently resides will be taken over by complete gang control.

Pastor Maxeau and I agreed to make contact every three hours with the use of a code word. It has now been eight hours since I have received an update from him. His wife, affectionately referred to as "Mommy Anne", reached out to me to say she is relying on Psalm 91. She specifically cited Psalm 91:7 which states, *"Though a thousand fall at your side, though ten thousand are dying around you, these evils will not touch you."* I am overwhelmingly moved by Mommy Anne's faith in the Lord's protection.

I have known Pastor Maxeau since December of 2011. I met him during my first trip to Haiti with my family. You can read all about this trip in my first book *Peanut Butter Crackers and Flip Flops*. I have grown to love Maxeau and his wife as my very own family. As a matter of fact, their son, Fred, is living in our home in America. He is a special part of our family!

Besides my husband, I cannot think of anyone I trust more than Maxeau.

Maxeau is one of the godliest men I know. He is the person who taught me to see miracles and what it meant to be baptized by the Holy Spirit. He accompanied me in leading a voodoo priest to the Lord. He translated for me when we led a voodoo princess and her fiancé to the Lord. He was on the stage with me when the little boy who couldn't walk received the miracle of walking. We have gone through some of the most miraculous and difficult times of our lives together. I would not be writing this book, nor do I believe I would have had the opportunity to experience any of these miracles first hand, if it were not for Pastor Maxeau Antoine. I pray this book and the real experiences I have witnessed will have the same impact on you that Pastor Maxeau has had on me. Because of my belief in God's supernatural power, I am able to sit here and type this dedication because I know God will use the hot mess in Haiti, and He will come in and perform a *miracle*.

Thank you, Maxeau, for all you have done and all you continue to do to care for the thousands of children in Haiti through Love Him Love Them's schools, churches, orphanages, vocational school, transition home, and hospital. You are an inspiration to me and everyone who meets you. Thank you for listening to God and being quick to obey Him even when you don't fully understand Him. You have lived out much of this story with me, and I am grateful to you for teaching me how to live an abundant life and giving me so much wisdom.

As I have written these last few words in great despair about the situation in Haiti, I have just received a message from Pastor Maxeau. It says, "I am safe for now. I just moved to another location. Our next step depends on God. Who knows how and what He will do to set us free from the gangs?" I encourage you to hold on to that because you and I are in our next steps as well. All of our next steps depend on God! If we depend on Him, we will be safe, and He will move us to our next location. He will set us free!

With Love,
Linda Gunter
Co-Founder and CEO of Love Him Love Them

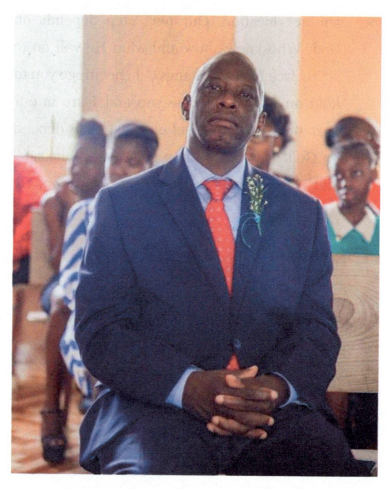
Pictured: Pastor Maxeau Antoine

(From left to right) Linda Gunter stands alongside "Mommy Anne" and Pastor Maxeau Antoine for a picture.

Table of Contents

09	Noel Collins: Editor and Co-Author	128	*Divine Intervention*
11	Forward	130	From Death to Life
15	Preface	135	The Bus
20	*God's Provision*	139	Hit and Run
22	Someone Gave Me a Minivan	147	Raped at Sixteen
29	The Multiplied Peanut Butter Crackers	154	*Spiritual Warfare*
36	Gang Roads Opening	156	Josey's Attitude Adjustment
41	A New Kidney!	162	Baptized By The Holy Spirit
44	In the Middle of the Storm	168	A Note to Readers
52	Redaphca's Ears	169	Jeremy's Story (Part One)
61	*Miraculous Healings*	175	Kenol and Lisa
		189	Jeremy's Story (Part Two)
63	Blind Eye Opened	204	The Ambulance Driver
69	Aicha Walks!	210	*Salvation*
76	Belinda's Brain	212	Little Girl Speaks
81	Susie's Lupus	218	Voodoo Request
86	A Healed Heart	224	Eldo's Baptism
91	Maria's Baby	228	The Pastor's Ex Wife Shows Up!
95	Jane's Infection	235	Joel's Salvation Story
99	Pink Eye Healed	242	*Joy*
107	*Obedience*	243	Eldo is 21!
108	A Word About Paperwork	249	A Miraculous Mountain of Mashed Potatoes
113	The X-Ray Machine	254	Belinda's Story
119	My Wedding Ring	259	A Wrinkled Napkin and A Determined Heart
125	Update on Jane	266	Path to Salvation
		269	Closing Statments

Noel Collins
Co-Author and Editor

For as long as I can remember, writing has been a passion of mine. As I became older and more firm in my Christian faith, it became clear to me that writing was a gift the Lord gave to me to use for His glory and kingdom. Even in seasons of disobedience when I did not write as often as the Lord called me to do, I would constantly feel the Holy Spirit impressing on me to write the things He had placed on my heart.

On December 18th of 2022, I felt a very strong conviction over my disobedience. I had not written in some time, and the Lord made it clear to me on that day that I was not using the gift of writing He had given me to further His kingdom. I quickly repented of my sin, and I asked God to provide an opportunity for me to write. I was unsure where He would lead me, but I was determined to walk in accordance to His will.

The very next day, I received a text from Linda Gunter. She shared with me that the Lord had impressed on her to write another book for her ministry, Love Him Love Them. In this book, she would focus on real-life miracle stories and accounts of the supernatural. She had every story pre-recorded on her YouTube channel and podcast; however, she just needed someone willing to write the stories out.

Tears filled my eyes as I read the text because I knew *this book* was the answer to my prayer from the night before. It has been such a blessing to write the miracles Linda has seen throughout her life and ministry, and my faith has grown significantly as I've written them. As you read, I pray that you will begin to ask for and see miracles in your everyday life. The Lord performs signs and wonders today, and He can do it for you!

Always Loving Him and Loving Them,
Noel Collins

Forward

I had the pleasure of meeting Linda many years ago as she walked into my showroom and asked, "How black are you?" I was quite shocked to hear that question coming from a southern Caucasian woman. My company is called African American Expressions, which was founded over thirty years ago and has grown to the largest of its kind in the world! Needless to say, in my thirty years of work, I had never come into contact with anyone quite like Linda! It was her introduction and charisma that intrigued me as she shared her passion for the hearts of the people her ministry serves. Soon after our introduction, I invited Linda to sit down to get to know her and her ministry, Love Him Love Them. When we met, she shared recent photos from Haiti, the country her ministry exists to serve. I listened to her tell stories of her time there, and

I fell in love with her work in Haiti. The story that brought tears to my eyes was of Linda finding an abandoned infant on the mountain who had no name. The Love Him Love Them ministry took in the beautiful baby and gave the infant a name.

I am reminded of James 1:27 when I think of Linda Gunter and Love Him Love Them. It reads, *"Religion that God our Father accepts as pure and faultless is this: to look after orphans and widows in their distress and to keep oneself from being polluted by the world."* Linda's work proves to be an ongoing challenge, especially since civil unrest has plagued the country of Haiti. However, God has always shown up and showed out, and He continues to combat the obstacles of the day. He is faithful! As you read *Miracles with Mommy Linda,* you will encounter many stories of Linda depending on the Holy Spirit and His Word to guide her through difficult circumstances. This book will encourage you to step out of your comfort zone and become an instrument for God's will!

John 14:12 states, *"Very truly I tell you, whoever believes in me will do the works I have been doing, and they will do even greater things than these, because I am going to the Father."* Miracles with Mommy Linda is proof that we are living in the time of greater works. Nothing is impossible for God! When we listen and obey the instructions given to us by the Holy Spirit, we can be used to further His kingdom! I have witnessed the demonstration and power of God at work in true believers. After studying the book of John, I discovered Jesus had mentioned the importance of believing over thirty times! Why did He mention this so much? Maybe Jesus knew it would be difficult for people to grasp the concept of believing. Jesus is the Word, and when we speak and release the Word guided by the Holy Spirit, miracles happen!

Miracles with Mommy Linda includes real life testimonies of how God moves in the lives of His people. Please be prayerful for the children of Haiti and the staff of Love Him Love Them as you read this book, and remember that God rewards those who diligently seek Him!

God Bless,
Greg Perkins

Greg Perkins
CEO of African American Expressions

Preface

Miracles in the Bible are referenced as "signs and wonders." Before you read *Miracles with Mommy Linda,* I want you to have a clear understanding of what a miracle is. The biblical definition of a miracle or sign and wonder is an event that involves the direct and mighty action of God. This occurrence can transcend the laws of nature and the social expectations of behaviors. Miracles can only be attributed to the supernatural work of God. Throughout the Bible, it is recorded that God uses miracles to reveal Himself, His character, and His purpose to His children through extraordinary occurrences that are not otherwise explainable.

A miracle can be performed by God or through a human instrument. Several different forms of miracles are revealed throughout the Bible. For example, God shows His divine control over nature through the parting of the Red Sea (Exodus 14:21-22). Many occurrences of instantaneous healings are recorded as well. An example of one of God's miraculous healings is seen when Jesus heals two blind men (Matthew 9:27-31). Miraculous exorcisms set people free from Satan's control and helped spread the good news of Jesus (Luke 4:31-37). Miracles of resurrection were proof of God's sovereignty and power (1 Kings 17:17-24).

Some may wonder why I am so fascinated with miracles and the supernatural power of God. In today's society, everyone seems to crave the supernatural, but not the supernatural power of the Lord. Let me be clear in saying that there is a distinct difference between miracles and manifestations. Miracles are from God. Demonic manifestations are from Satan. There is an ungodly supernatural realm in the world that exists of ouija boards, tarot cards, crystals, yoga, and the casting of spells. Many people believe there are good witches who aim to bring positive supernatural order to the world, but the Bible clearly states that we are not to *"..turn to mediums or seek out spiritists, for you will be defiled by them"* (Leviticus 19:31).

Satan is very crafty, and he finds ways to intervene in our culture. Astrology, horoscope readings, mandalas, telekinesis, and Reiki practices are works of Satan, not God. I encourage you to be aware of Satan's schemes. These ungodly elements can easily infiltrate your life and the lives of your children. Many popular shows presented to teenagers feature several of these elements. Please be aware of the content you are allowing to be seen and heard in your home. Live a life in accordance with the Word of God, which warns us to *"be alert and of sober mind. Your enemy the devil prowls around like a roaring lion looking for someone to devour"* (1 Peter 5:8).

After reading this book, you will be equipped to trust in the supernatural power of the Holy Spirit as you receive the miracles you ask Him to perform in your life. You can see miracles unfold before your eyes when you have complete faith in God's almighty power to perform them. In *Miracles with Mommy Linda*, you will find thirty-seven accounts of the miraculous. The Gospels record about thirty-seven miracles performed through Jesus. However, the apostle John stresses that these recorded miracles merely scratch the surface of all the miracles our Savior did (John 21:25). I could not fit all of the miracles I have seen in one book, so I am releasing a *Miracles with Mommy Linda* devotional book in December of 2023. This book will include exclusive stories that have not been included in the following pages. If the stories in *Miracles with Mommy Linda* build your faith, I encourage you to prayerfully consider purchasing the devotional after its release. I can assure you that your confidence in God's supernatural power will grow significantly!

Always Remembering to Love Him and Love Them,
Linda Gunter
Co-Founder and CEO of Love Him Love Them

Chapter One: God's Provision

"And my God will meet all your needs according to the riches of His glory in Christ Jesus." -Philipians 4:19

In this chapter, you will read of miraculous encounters that happened as a result of God's provision. The Lord cares for us with an unexplainable love of a Father, and He *provides* for His children in miraculous ways every day! As you read this chapter, I encourage you to look back on moments of your life when the Lord provided for a need of yours. As you think about these moments, thank God for His faithfulness and for meeting your needs. My heart's desire is that your faith will be built as you read, and you will gain the confidence to trust in God's provision over your life. He *will* meet all of your needs according to

His will, and that is something to be thankful for!

Someone Gave Me a Free Minivan!

One of the many events that Love Him Love Them hosts throughout the year is our annual Thanksgiving Day event. During this event, we plate thousands of Thanksgiving meals to be sent out all over the state of Georgia. After we finish plating the meals, we begin delivering the meals in person to those in need. While I was out delivering meals after this particular Thanksgiving event, I was led to the home of a mother with seven kids. After handing the mother her Thanksgiving meals, I decided to sit down with her to get to know her story. Through our conversation, I learned that her husband was in jail. It was then that I knew this was a divine intervention because Love Him Love Them also provides an annual *Night of Hope* event for children with an incarcerated parent to receive a night of food, Christmas gifts, games, and more! I nonchalantly asked the young woman if she had any plans during the Christmas season. She replied, "Oh no. We are just waiting for my husband to get out of jail."

I encouraged her and the children to join us at our upcoming *Night of Hope* to ensure that her kids would have a Christmas to remember for years to come. I explained to her that the ministry would provide all the Christmas gifts for the children. Immediately, tears began to stream down her face as she said, "Gifts for the children?" The lady then began to tell me about how she did not have the means to provide her seven children with Christmas gifts. She shared that she had lost her job at the local Waffle House due to her car breaking down, and she had no means of transportation to get to work. During times like this, she typically depended on her husband to fix up the car. However, that would not be an option for a while due to his recent incarceration. She was able to get a mechanic to look at her car, but the cost to fix it would be over $1,000! The woman appreciated my invitation to the event, but she was concerned about not having a ride to bring the children to the *Night of Hope*. My automatic thought was, "Girl, you don't need a car, you need a BUS with all of those kiddos!" Needless to say, I left the busy home wondering how Love Him Love Them could best serve this precious family in need.

Five days prior to our *Night of Hope*, a couple my husband and I met during Love Him Love Them's Haitian Orphan Children's Choir tour showed up at our doorstep unannounced. In my confusion as to why this couple came to my home, I invited them to sit at the dining room table. After we sat down, the wife told me, "Linda, we have been trying to sell our minivan for eight months. Every time we try to sell a vehicle, we park it in the same spot, a place with lots of traffic coming though, and we have never had a vehicle parked out there for longer than an hour!" Then, she explained that she and her husband had a conversation. They believed the minivan they had parked in this very specific spot had not sold because *I* needed it. The sweet mother of seven kids that I met on Thanksgiving Day immediately came to my mind. She needed a vehicle! The couple looked up at me and said, "Well.. do you need a minivan?" I looked at my husband and then back to the couple sitting across from us at the dining room table, and I said, "I don't, but I know who does." I then shared with the couple the story of the lady with seven children, and as we sat at the table crying, the couple handed over the keys to me. As we walked out to see the minivan, I assumed it would be junked up because it had not sold. I could not have been more wrong. The minivan was beautiful, inside and out! This sweet couple left my home that night taking absolutely nothing in return for the minivan. That's right, it was given to me completely free!

Five days later, the same woman I met on Thanksgiving Day brought her seven children to our *Night of Hope* event, and Love Him Love Them was able to gift her with a free, beautiful minivan! What a miracle! This gift caused a ripple effect in the ways Love Him Love Them could best support this family. Due to the woman being out of work, she was soon to lose her home with the Housing Authority. Our ministry was able to find this woman a job to which she could now commute, and we pleaded her case with the Housing Authority. Because of God's provision, the eviction notice was dismissed, and they were able to enjoy their new vehicle together.

The following year, this precious family decided to come to the *Night of Hope* as volunteers to serve other families in need. To my surprise, the woman I met the previous year stood up in front of everyone and shared about how the Lord provided. She was without a car, jobless, almost homeless, and had a husband in jail, but *God provided.* Not only did the Lord provide every need, but her husband, who was previously incarcerated, came to the event with her! They showed up to the event, seven kids in tow, in the same minivan God provided the year before. Both husband and wife had jobs and had recently moved into a new home! I do not know how many miracles this is in just one story, but I want to thank the couple who came to my house that night. Because they had a heart to see the Father's will unfold in a miraculous way, Love Him Love Them was able to serve this very special family during the Christmas season.

Pictured: The recipient family of the minivan gathers around Santa Claus during Love Him Love Them's annual *Night of Hope* event.

Scan the QR code to hear Linda Gunter share this story on YouTube!
Episode Title: " The Miracle of Hope: A Couple Showed up at my Door and Gave me a FREE Minivan"

The Multiplied Peanut Butter Crackers!

What you are about to read tells the story of the very first miracle I personally witnessed the Lord perform. I never could have imagined that this initial life event would lead to hundreds of miracles in my life! Needless to say, I had no idea what the Lord had in store for me.

In 2004, my life changed in the most drastic way anyone could ever imagine a life to change. My best friend was brutally murdered by her husband. Her mother was also murdered that very same night, also by the hands of my friend's husband. Five beautiful children were left behind without parents as they witnessed their mother, grandmother, and father be taken away from them, all in one night. These children went on to live with their grandfather in New York, and they lived with him for about two years.

One day, I received a phone call from the grandfather of these children. He explained to me that he was terminally ill, and he needed to find a home for all five children, as soon as possible. He had called family members, friends, and anyone else he could think to call. He stated that I was his very last call before reaching out to social services to put the children in foster care, where they would most likely be separated from one another. My immediate response to this man was, "Absolutely not! I cannot take on five kids! I don't even really think I like kids all that much!" My husband overheard our conversation, and he was quick to correct my disagreeable response. He reminded me of James 1:27 in the Bible, which says, *"Religion that God our Father accepts as pure and faultless is this: to look after orphans and widows in their distress and to keep oneself from being polluted by the world.*" Even in my uncertainty, I was submissive to my husband's wisdom, and most importantly, to the Word of God. That day, the seventh day of the seventh month in the year of 2007 to be exact, my family of two grew to a family of seven.

~

Now is the perfect time to mention that the five children my husband and I took in as our own all those years ago are Haitian! In 2011, my husband and I decided to take the children on a mission trip to Haiti. I had never been on a mission trip before, so I was reading and soaking up all the information I could about Haiti and the community we would be serving prior to the trip. The guest house in Haiti where we stayed during that first trip was "My Father's Guest House." Interestingly enough, Love Him Love Them now runs that very same guest house! In the paperwork, it was mentioned that breakfast and dinner would be served at the guest house. However, during the day, we would be out and about in the community doing mission work, so we were responsible for bringing our own lunch and snacks in between the two meals served. I quickly went into mom-mode and packed those not so appetizing packets of tuna fish and crackers to have for lunch and peanut butter crackers for snacking. I calculated everything to a tee to ensure that there would be three packets of peanut butter crackers for each of us per day to have for snacks- no more, no less.

When we arrived at the guest house, little Haitian children came and started to knock on the gate. My daughters quickly went outside to greet the children with the manager of the home. They invited the children in, and what they did next sent me into panic mode. They started giving out the peanut butter crackers that I had accounted for to be our snacks for the week! Not only did they give out our snacks that very first day in Haiti, but when we first went out into the community to do mission work, they packed the crackers in their bookbags and passed them out to children on the street! My husband took notice of the snacks they were giving away and asked our children to stop passing out the packs of crackers I had spent time counting out for them.

As silly as it sounds, I started to think to myself, "Oh my goodness. We probably only have about two days worth of snack crackers left! What are we going to do for the remainder of the week?" I know my husband and I are probably the only parents in the world who have children who do this, but our kids did not listen to us! They *continued* to pass out those peanut butter crackers! The original Haitian kiddos that came to the gate that very first day showed up every day, and the girls gave them more and more crackers each time they came! Every morning when we would come downstairs in the guest house, there were still peanut butter crackers available. How was this possible? The girls were giving these things out left and right! We got down to the last couple days of the trip, and there were still packs of peanut butter crackers that we would find around the guest house. There were even a couple *cases* of crackers laying around, not just the individual packs. I finally asked my husband, David, "What gives with these silly peanut butter crackers?" He said, "Linda, somehow they are...*multiplying*."

We ended up heading back to the States and leaving the guest house behind with more peanut butter crackers than we originally came with. That first miracle in Haiti grew my faith more than I could have ever imagined! Now, when I find myself in a situation where food needs to be multiplied to feed the many we serve in our ministry, I look back and thank God for multiplying something as simple as peanut butter crackers. My heart's desire is that you will see that God is a wonder-working God, and He can work in the simple, mundane things in life. He did it for my family and those sweet Haitian children, and I have no doubt that He can do it for you!

Scan the QR code to hear Linda Gunter share this story on YouTube!

** To learn more about how The Gunters' planned their very first family trip to Haiti and their experiences during the mission trip, please read Linda's first-written book, *Peanut Butter Crackers and Flip Flops*. To order, visit www.lovehimlovethem.org. **

Gang Roads Opening

Love Him Love Them has several ministries across our six locations in the country of Haiti. We have orphanages, schools, churches, a jewelry line, and a hospital, to name a few. Since 2021, Love Him Love Them has experienced great difficulty in getting food and medical supplies to several of our locations. Due to the increased gang activity and civil unrest since the assassination of Haiti's president, the roads to many of our ministry's locations are blocked off by the very prominent and violent 400 Mawozo gang. Love Him Love Them partners with Feed The Hunger in feeding over 5,000 children every day in our schools, orphanages, and hospitals, and it is important that our shipment containers of food are delivered on time.

There has been a lot of frustration surrounding the situation in Haiti. One of the reasons for this is because we had a container full of medical supplies and food already sent to the country of Haiti to be dispersed amongst our six locations. However, due to the road blockings by the 400 Mawozo gang, we were unable to get the food and medical supplies to any of our locations. It is important to mention that our schools and orphanages were going on twenty-eight days of having no food when this particular miracle took place. In previous attempts to bring food or other supplies through the roadblocks, the gang members would stop our vehicles and take any food or supplies we had.

~

I was at a Haitian attorney's office in Chamblee, Georgia working on visa paperwork for my kids. Unbeknownst to me, this attorney's office had a designated prayer time every day at noon. I just so happened to be talking with an attorney during that time, and when the clock hit 12:00PM, the attorney working with me asked if I would like to join the other employees and herself in a time of prayer. Of course, I quickly agreed and followed her into the board room, which was filled with many employees.

Before the time of prayer began, I found myself wrestling with the fact that we could not get food or medical supplies to any of our locations in Haiti. It hurt my heart knowing the children, teachers, doctors, and nurses under Love Him Love Them's ministries were going on a month of having no food or medical supplies. I began to tearfully share this information with the attorneys in hopes that they would lift up our dear friends in Haiti in prayer. We sang and prayed together in the boardroom for thirty-eight minutes, and as I cried and prayed, I witnessed those mighty men and women of God join me in fervent prayer for those in

Haiti. The Lord reminded me of James 5:16 in that moment, which says, "*..the effectual and fervent prayer of a righteous man availeth much.*" There was something so special about praying alongside like-minded people. These men and women knew exactly why my heart ached so much for the country of Haiti because theirs were aching just as much, if not even more so than my own, because of their Haitian heritage. They completely understood the evil that was taking place in Haiti, the kind of evil that was keeping starving orphans from being fed.

After the prayer meeting, I finished up the paperwork I originally came to the office to complete that day. As I was heading out to my car to head back home, I looked down at my phone and noticed I missed a notification from one of our Haitians on the ground at 12:11PM. The message sent to me at that time read, "Linda! Great news! The gangs, for a reason no one can understand, decided to open up the roads today to allow us to get our food and medical supplies through!" The joy that filled me was unexplainable as I thanked God for answering our very specific prayer just moments ago in the little boardroom! I ran back into the attorney's office yelling, "They opened up the roads! They opened up the roads!" The employees before me had tears of absolute joy streaming down their faces as they realized the Lord had answered our prayers. Because of the Lord's provision in answering our fervent prayers, the Haitians in our care were able to receive desperately needed food and medical supplies that day. What a blessing!

Scan the QR code to hear Linda Gunter share this story on YouTube!

A New Kidney!

James 5:14 says, "*Is anyone among you sick? He must call the spiritual leaders of the church, and they are to pray over him- anointing him with oil in the name of the Lord. And the prayer of faith will restore the one who is sick. The Lord will raise him up. If they have sinned, they will be forgiven.*" Additionally, in Psalms 107:20, it is stated that we can "*send forth healing.*" The first verse mentioned speaks of anointing and praying over someone sick in person. The following verse explains that we can send forth healing, regardless of whether or not the person in need of healing is in the same room with us.

I had a phone conversation with a woman named Keshawn who had a husband in need of a kidney. Believe it or not, Keshawn never prayed for her husband's kidney to be healed. However, she did pray that he could get onto a list to receive a new kidney. She had been praying this prayer for over five years! Because Keshawn and her husband were in another state, I prayed in Psalms 107:20 fashion and "sent forth healing" over the phone! After we prayed together, she began to share with me that her husband had been to numerous doctors and underwent several different procedures in hopes of qualifying for a kidney donor list. However, they had been unsuccessful thus far.

Two days after this phone call, Keshawn called me back and said, "Linda, you are not going to believe this! We just left the dialysis place, and they put my husband on the list!" I responded with, "Well, that's what we prayed for, right!?" She then told me that not only did they place him on the list, but he was placed as number one on the list! Her husband would be the very next recipient of a kidney! She continued by saying, "It's almost as if we had God's favor!"

Of course, my immediate response was, "Of course we have God's favor! That is *exactly* what we prayed for!"

Keshawn and I were so thankful that the Lord answered our prayers and provided a way for her husband to receive healing through a new kidney. My prayer for you is that you will have the boldness to ask God for whatever you are in need of, just Like Keshawn did for her husband, and *trust* in Him to answer your prayers.

Scan the QR code to hear Linda Gunter share this story on YouTube!
Episode Title: "Miracles with Mommy Linda- Keshawn's Kidney"

In the Middle of the Storm

In 2016, during Love Him Love Them's second tour with the Haitian Orphan Children's Choir, we found ourselves in Ft. Lauderdale, Florida at a Haitian church to perform a concert. The following day after the concert, we were scheduled to fly all thirty Haitian children from the choir directly back to Haiti. Throughout the concert, I felt my cell phone in my back pocket vibrate over and over again. Thank goodness I had it on vibrate! After the children sang, I pulled my phone out and realized I had thirty emails from Delta Airlines informing me that all flights to Haiti had been canceled due to Hurricane Matthew. Haiti was in the direct path of this upcoming devastation of a storm. I immediately started to panic. The home office in the United States for Love Him Love Them is in Northeast Georgia, and we were all the way in Ft. Lauderdale, Florida! All of our ministry's volunteers were planning to drive back home that night, and I was going to be the only adult available to fly with the children back to Haiti the following day. Not to mention, the country I had grown to love so dearly was in the direct path of a hurricane!

I quickly pulled aside five of the choir's musicians and asked if they knew what was happening in Haiti. Our drummer began to tell me that he had talked with several of his friends back in Haiti, and they were preparing for the upcoming storm headed their way. He continued by saying, "We need to pray. Now." At that moment, I sat alongside the five musicians on the stage, and we prayed for the country of Haiti. After we prayed, I said, "Now what are we going to do!?"

To add to my panic, I realized that the children's visas were about to expire. We were scheduled to fly back to Haiti that Monday, and their visas were expiring the following Wednesday. If we could not get those kids back to Haiti by Wednesday, they would officially be in the United States illegally and could be in danger of being deported. If this happened, they would no longer be allowed to come back to the States. I had no idea what to do. Thankfully, the children were set up to stay with different host families for the night, so I had the entire night to myself to talk with Delta Airlines on the phone to come up with a solution. After hours on the phone, my worst fears were confirmed. The airport was completely shut down, and there would be absolutely no flights out to Haiti until further notice. Of course, in my desperation, I called my sweet husband. He told me that by the next day, I needed to head back up to Georgia with the choir so we could be closer to our ministry's resources. I agreed that this was my only option, and I tried my best to get at least a little bit of sleep before making the eleven-hour drive back to Georgia with thirty Haitian kids!

The following morning, when I went out to start the bus for the choir, the bus would not crank! Immediately, I threw my hands up and said, "ARE YOU KIDDING ME?!" The bus had to be towed to the closest mechanic. However, the part needed to fix the bus would not be available until the next day. In my frustration, I called the pastor of the church where the choir had performed the night before and asked him if there was any way we could sleep on the floor at his church for one night. Graciously, the pastor agreed to offer us space to stay. The following day, we were able to get the bus back, and as we headed back to Georgia, we continued to hear news of how Hurricane Matthew was destroying the Caribbean.

A few hours into our trip back to Georgia, you won't believe it, the engine in the van carrying our luggage blew! We had to pull over to the side of the road and unhook the luggage trailer to have the van towed. I could not believe we were having this much trouble! We were still so far away from home, and I needed a place, yet again, for the children to stay at for the night. My husband graciously gifted us with his Holiday Inn points so we could book a hotel in Valdosta, Georgia for the night. Later that evening, I got on my knees to pray. I said, "God, I have absolutely no idea what I am supposed to do. We have a broken down van. We just got the choir bus fixed. We are completely out of money for food to feed the children. I just do not know what to do, Lord." I quickly remembered I had a friend who lived in the area where we were stranded. I called her, and she agreed to pay to feed the children at Chick-Fil-A the following day.

The next morning, we swept the entire continental breakfast buffet out at the Holiday

Inn, and I stuffed whatever extra bananas and muffins I could find into my bag to have for the rest of the trip home! Before we left, the children had a moment to swim in the hotel's pool. As I watched them having the time of their lives playing in the water, I couldn't help but think about how their home country was being destroyed by water. There was no telling what devastation they would eventually return to.

During the very slim moments of free time I had during the hectic trip, I would make phone calls to news stations in an effort to get some sort of help as we were stranded. We were able to get media coverage, and a man named Tony Holtzclaw from Dawsonville, Georgia heard on the radio that Love Him Love Them's Haitian Orphan Children's Choir was stranded in Valdosta, Georgia. Tony called me and asked where we were. I told him that we were in Valdosta and explained all the trials we had endured over the last couple of days. I was in shock when the next thing he said was, "Send me your address. I'm on the way. My church here in Dawsonville is already collecting and preparing food and setting up air mattresses. The choir is welcome to stay at the church for as long as you need." He proceeded to tell me that he was bringing a bus for the kids and a tow truck to bring the broken down van back home for us. Pastor Tony Holtzclaw and Harmony Baptist Church in Dawsonville, Georgia rescued all of us that day. The choir was able to stay at the church for a week and a half. Even now, years after this crazy experience, when asked about their favorite church, all thirty Haitian children from the choir speak so highly of Harmony Baptist. The Lord provided us with the miracle of this church community, and we are forever grateful for the kindness they showed us during our time with them.

Pictured: The team from Harmony Baptist Church arrives to rescue the choir and vehicles!

Scan the QR code to hear Linda Gunter share this story on YouTube!
Episode Title: "Miracles with Mommy Linda- In the Middle of the Storm"

You can read more about the many miracles Love Him Love Them's Haitian Orphan Children's Choir experienced in Linda Gunter's *Choir of Angels: How 30 Orphans Changed Their World*. To order, visit www.lovehimlovethem.org.

Redaphca's Ears

Many of the original choir members from Love Him Love Them's Haitian Orphan Children's Choir remain in the United States on F-1 student visas. Redaphca is one of the children from the choir, and she resides in the States with a host family while she attends college. It is such a blessing to have her around!

As a gift from her host family, Redaphca had the opportunity to get her ears pierced. About twenty days after receiving the piercing, keloids (overgrowths of scar tissue) began to form on her ears. As days passed, the keloids continued to grow larger and larger. I received a phone call from her host parents, and together we found a doctor to treat Redaphca's ears.

The doctor we found prescribed a series of shots to help with the keloids. Unfortunately, the COVID-19 pandemic hit in the midst of Redaphca's treatment, and she was unable to go back to the doctor to finish the series of shots needed to treat the keloids. Additionally, Redaphca had to move to another host family due to circumstances out of her control. Soon after the move, I became in charge of finding her the medical attention she needed for her ears.

~

One day, I received a phone call from the office of a plastic surgeon. It had come to their attention that the ministry was shipping a container to Haiti, and they wanted to make a donation of office dividers to be sent to Love Him Love Them's "Valley of Hope" hospital in Haiti. Of course, I gladly accepted the offer. When I hung up the phone, I thought to myself, "Hmmm.. plastic surgeons.. could they possibly help me with Redaphca's ears?"

I called back, and asked, "Have y'all ever heard of keloids?" I'm sure my question had everyone laughing on the other end, but I was desperate to find help for Redaphca. I explained the situation over the phone, and to my surprise, the plastic surgeon, Dr. Meadows said, "Absolutely! We would love to help Redaphca, and we want to do it pro bono." I was so excited to share the amazing news with Redaphca! Then, it was explained to me that Dr. Meadows from Meadows Surgical Arts founded an organization alongside his wife called, "The Surgical Hope Foundation". This non-profit organization helped in providing outpatient surgical services at no cost to patients in need. Dr. Meadows so kindly decided to utilize the funds from The Surgical Hope Foundation to cover the costs of Redaphca's procedure.

When I took Redaphca in for a pre-op appointment, Dr. Meadows assured us that he could remove the keloids. However, after the surgery, Redaphca would need radiation treatment. The radiation could not be completed within Dr. Meadow's office, so I soon found myself calling around to many different radiation centers in hopes of finding someone willing to help Redaphca. Eventually, Dr. Meadows found the University Cancer and Blood Center in Athens, Georgia, and he referred Redaphca there for treatment. Soon after, I brought Redaphca to the UCBC for a consultation.

As I sat down with the financial aid department of the UCBC, I shared Redaphca's story. I explained that medical care for the choir children from Haiti could be expensive for the ministry, and we were desperate to find someone willing to help. After hearing Redaphca's story, the financial aid employee decided to waive the $150 consultation fee, and she sent us on our way to a room to wait for a doctor.

After the consultation, the physician, Dr. Terri, was confident in providing the radiation treatment needed for Redaphca's ears. However, four rounds of radiation was going to cost about $15,000! Again, I explained Redaphca's situation. I said, "Redaphca has a pro bono case with Dr. Meadows for the procedure on her ears. We were hoping to have a similar case here as well." Unfortunately, it was made clear to us that Redaphca would not be taken on as a pro bono patient through the UCBC. We left the consultation, and jokingly I said, "Sorry, Redaphca! You're going to have some big ears for a while! $15,000 is insane!" Although we laughed together at the joke, we were still disappointed and wanted to know the next steps it would take to get Redaphca the help she needed.

Shortly after the consultation, I received a phone call. It was from Dr. Terri with the

University Cancer and Blood Center. He said, "Linda, I just want you to know that we will do the radiation pro bono." I couldn't believe it! Dr. Meadows was unwilling to complete the surgery if a plan for radiation was not lined up. After praying with Redaphca for the Lord to provide radiation treatment at little to no cost, we got *exactly* what we prayed for!

As you can see in the pictures below, Redaphca received the procedure and radiation needed to treat the keloids on her ears. We are so thankful to Dr. Meadows and Dr. Terri for providing this much needed treatment at no cost! The Lord provided these two doctors for Redaphca, and we are so thankful for His divine provision!

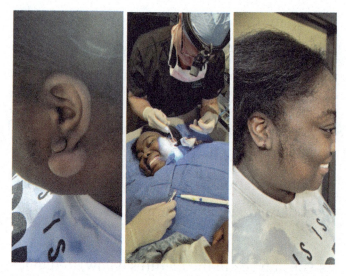

(From left to right) Redaphca has large keloids on her earlobes. Dr. Meadows performs surgery to remove the keloids. Redaphca smiles for a photo after receiving the surgery on her ears.

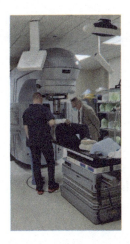

Pictured: Dr. Terri from the University Cancer and Blood Center stands over Redaphca as she receives radiation treatment.

(From left to right) Linda poses for a picture with Redaphca and Dr. Terri after Redaphca received radiation treatment free of cost!

Scan the QR code to hear Linda Gunter share
this story on YouTube!

Chapter Two: Miraculous Healings

"Is anyone among you sick? Let them call the elders of the church to pray over them and anoint them with oil in the name of the Lord. And the prayer offered in faith will make the sick person well; the Lord will raise them up. If they have sinned, they will be forgiven."
James 5:14-15

When we think about miracles performed by Jesus, it is very easy to refer to miracles of healing. He healed the woman with internal bleeding (Mark 5:25-26), a crippled man (John 5:2-9), and a man born blind (John 9:1-7), to name a few. It is easy for us to find encouragement through these accounts when we read the Bible, but oftentimes, we may find it difficult to believe that God still heals today!

As you read this chapter filled with miraculous healings, I pray that your faith will be built as you gain the confidence to ask God to heal you and your loved ones of any and all sickness and disease. Our Father in Heaven wants to see his children healed. Trust in that beautiful truth today!

Blind Eye Opened

After completing two tours with Love Him Love Them's Haitian Orphan Children's Choir, twenty-two of the thirty Haitian children in the choir were able to stay in the United States on student visas. Out of the twenty-two choir kids remaining in the States, there were six girls who lived with host families near me. Even through a global pandemic and other life challenges, the Lord made a way for me to join these six girls on another tour to surrounding churches and events. We called this precious group of young ladies, the "Loved by Him Girls", and we toured for an entire year!

One of the churches the Loved By Him Girls visited was in Bogart, Georgia. They entered the church with the same expectation they had entering all the churches we visited throughout our year-long tour together. They wanted to pray for the kids from the choir who had to return back to Haiti. The girls' desire was to help raise funds to send back to their choir friends in Haiti, many of whom were either in an orphanage or going through vocational school. Those six Haitian girls may have been small in number, but their testimonies and singing voices were mighty in the Lord in the small- town church that day!

After the service, there was an altar call, and I explained to the church members that the Haitian Orphan Children's Choir typically spread out amongst the congregation to pray over individuals. Of course, this took place when there were thirty children in the choir. Now that there were just six girls, we asked those in need of prayer to come up to one of the six, and whoever they walked up to would be more than willing to pray for any and all prayer requests. I continued to share with the congregation that I had witnessed marriages healed, finances restored, addictions broken, and seen many other miraculous accounts happen after these precious children prayed over people. I had no doubt in my mind that the Lord could show up again through those girls in the little church in Bogart, Georgia that morning.

To my disbelief, no one came for prayer after the altar call. This very rarely happened at any of the churches the choir visited, so I was taken aback for a moment. Then, the Holy Spirit encouraged me to make another altar call, and I said, "If you are here today, and you are sick, or if you know of someone who is sick, we would love for you to come receive prayer." From what I can recall, two or three individuals came to the altar for prayer, and the six girls hovered around them to pray. While the girls prayed, a lady walked down to the front of the church. She came to me and explained that she was seventy-eight years old and blind in her right eye. I immediately went to reach for the anointing oil in my purse because I remembered James 5:14 in the Bible, which says, *"Is anyone among you sick? Let them call the elders of the church to pray over them and anoint them with oil in the name of the Lord"*. I proceeded to anoint this woman with oil, and I prayed over her. After I prayed, I asked her to cover her left eye and look at the banner I had at a nearby product table for our *Beauty for Ashes* jewelry line. I said, "Can you see what that banner says?" She told me she still could not see anything out of her right eye. I did the only thing I knew to do at that moment. I prayed again! After the second prayer, I asked her to cover her left eye once again to check if she had regained sight in the right eye. The woman *still* could not see out of one eye. I was starting to get slightly disappointed, but I looked over and noticed the girls had finished praying over the few church members at the altar. I called Redaphca and Belinda, two of the

Haitian girls, over to pray for the woman with me. Shortly after I called them over, I was pulled in another direction to pray over another individual.

Not even a minute after being directed over to someone else, I heard the elderly woman screaming, "I can see! I can see!" Belinda and Redaphca were smiling ear to ear saying, "Really!? You can see!?" I ran over to look at the lady's eye, and it looked like she had a brand new right eye! It was almost as if an angel came down from Heaven and gifted her with a new one! She was healed! I was so glad that I leaned into the Holy Spirit and asked those girls to join me in prayer instead of quitting after the first and second prayer attempts. If I would have quit, that precious woman may not have received healing that day!

I want to encourage you to walk in boldness and be an instrument for God in His healing of others. Even if it takes two or three times, don't stop praying! If you need to rally up prayer partners to join you in praying for healing, do it! Satan wants us to lose faith in divine healing, but God wants us to be confident in Him as we *expect* miraculous healings in our lives!

Scan the QR code to hear Linda Gunter share this story on YouTube!
Episode Title: "Miracles with Mommy Linda- Blind Eye Opened"

Aicha Walks!

My dear friend, Dr. Trudy Simmons, is the Executive Producer and Host of *The Christian View* television show. One day, she graciously invited me to come on her show in West Palm Beach, Florida to share about one of Love Him Love Them's books called *Choir of Angels: How 30 Orphans Changed Their World*. Of course, I NEVER pass up an opportunity to go to the beach, so I quickly accepted her invitation!

We decided to take a flight to Florida, and before our travels, we had a two-hour delay in the Atlanta airport. To pass the time, I started a casual conversation with a man sitting near me. I asked him why he was heading to West Palm Beach, and he explained to me that his wife and daughter had been in that area for the last two years, and they were waiting for his arrival. At the time, he was living in Michigan, but he had a layover in Atlanta. In my bluntness, I said, "That's kind of strange. Your wife and kid are down in Florida, and you are all the way up in Michigan!" He laughed at my comment and told me that his daughter was in need of intensive physical therapy and surgery for a disability affecting her legs. He and his wife found the best care for his daughter in West Palm Beach, so that is exactly where his wife took her while he stayed in Michigan to work. He continued by saying that he would visit them as often as he could.

After I listened to his story, I told the man that Love Him Love Them had a 24-hour prayer team, and I wanted to have the team pray for his daughter and family. He was very thankful for the offer, and he accepted. I asked him what his daughter's name was, and he replied, "Her name is Aicha." To be honest, I was a little shocked by this response. The man I was talking with was very obviously Caucasian, and because I worked so closely with the Haitian Orphan Children's Choir, I could tell his daughter had a beautiful name that would most likely be heard in a country outside of the United States. Apparently, my face didn't hide my shock very well because he laughed again and explained that his daughter was from the Ivory Coast in Africa, and Aicha was in the United States on a student visa.

The man proceeded to tell me the extent of his daughter's disability. Aicha was born with her feet backwards, and her hands also had some deformities. She was unable to use her hands or feet properly, so she was wheelchair bound. I couldn't even begin to imagine the challenges this family had walked through. Then, I asked the man if I could meet up with his family in West Palm Beach so I could lay hands on Aicha and pray over her. I told him about the miraculous healings I had witnessed before, and I knew God could perform a miraculous healing in Aicha as well. Without hesitation, he made arrangements for his wife and daughter to meet us at the airport in West Palm Beach.

When we arrived at our destination, I walked out to the pickup area at the airport with Trudy and the man I talked with previously. Of course, it was very chaotic, and there were many security officers rushing people to make way for new traffic. We quickly huddled into the parked van on the curb with the man's daughter. His wife came out of the van and walked around to where we were with tears streaming down her face. She said to me, "Oh my goodness. I have no idea who you are, but I feel like I have known you my entire life!" I explained to her that the Holy Spirit orchestrated this meeting, and we proceeded to pray over Aicha.

The following day, I invited the family to my hotel, and I prayed over Aicha again. After that second prayer, Aicha still was unable to walk. I left the hotel feeling a little saddened that Aicha did not experience a miraculous healing, but I had confidence that the Lord would continue to do a good work in this family.

~

Thirty-five days after this encounter with Aicha, I received a phone call from her parents. They said "Linda! Aicha was able to ring the victory bell at physical therapy today! She is now standing *and* walking!" As we both cried tears of joy on the phone together for what the Lord had done, the couple proceeded to tell me that they would be moving back up to Michigan. On their way back home, they wanted to stop in Atlanta to see me and give Love Him Love Them all of the medical supplies they had been using for Aicha to go towards our hospital in Haiti! What a blessing! Shortly after this phone conversation, my husband and I met the family as they passed through Atlanta to receive such a beautiful gift for the nurses, doctors, and patients in our hospital in Haiti.

I am thrilled to say that Aicha is back at school in Michigan, and she is still walking! She is a happy young girl who was healed by God in her time of need. I have no doubt the Lord can do the same for you! If you or someone you know is experiencing any type of ailment, I encourage you to remember Aicha's story. Trust that the same God who healed her can heal you and your loved ones too!

Pictured: Aicha rings the victory bell at her physical therapy appointment!

Scan the QR code to hear Linda Gunter share this story on YouTube!

Belinda's Brain

To read Belinda's origin story, please refer to Chapter Seven: Joy.

The following miraculous encounter happened to one of the precious girls from Love Him Love Them's Haitian Orphan Children's Choir, and her name is Belinda. After the choir tour, Belinda had the opportunity to stay in the United States on a student visa, and she stayed with a host family in South Georgia. During her time with this family, she began experiencing frequent seizures. When I first heard news of this, I was unsure if Belinda was facing a medical problem or a spiritual warfare problem. The reason why I say this is because in the country of Haiti, demonic manifestations often reveal themselves in a way that is very similar to epileptic seizures. However, to rule out a medical issue, Belinda's host family decided to take her to a doctor.

After many tests and scans, the doctor determined that Belinda had fluid leaking from her cerebellum! More tests and scans needed to be done to determine a plan of treatment, but shortly after Belinda's diagnosis, the COVID-19 pandemic hit. Due to the chaos that quickly affected the medical field, it became increasingly difficult for Belinda to receive consistent treatment. In addition to this, Belinda's host dad passed away due to complications from COVID-19. Because of this, she had to leave South Georgia and move to North Georgia with a new host family. Belinda had to start from square one and find a new neurologist in the area who was willing to take on her case and treatment. Due to her medical history, the newly found doctor had Belinda go through all the tests and scans for a second time to determine a proper treatment plan. The doctor determined *again* that Belinda's brain was leaking fluid, and she would need medication to stop the seizures she was experiencing.

Meanwhile, Belinda was touring with the Loved By Him Girls, which was a group of Haitian girls from Love Him Love Them's original Haitian Orphan Children's Choir. If you remember from the "Blind Eye Opened" account in the Miraculous Healings chapter, Belinda was the young girl who prayed over the woman to receive healing in her blind eye. Needless to say, Belinda had personally witnessed others receive miraculous healings before her own eyes. She was expectantly waiting for God to heal her next! It came to my attention that after all this time, *no one* had prayed over Belinda. It broke my heart to know that such a simple act of faith and obedience had been neglected. I quickly found my anointing oil and alongside a few others, we anointed and prayed over Belinda for the healing of her brain.

Shortly after this prayer for healing, Belinda returned back to the neurologist for further scans and tests. When the results from those tests came back, Belinda could not believe it. There were no signs of fluid leaking from her brain! Praise God! Everyone in the room, including the doctor, were shocked beyond belief. The doctor stated, "I can only describe this as being a *miracle."* Just a few days prior, it was determined that Belinda would need surgery to correct the leak, but now she was completely healed! I want to encourage you to not delay in praying for those in need of healing. I still do not understand how I missed out on several opportunities to pray over Belinda and her brain. Please do not be bound to what a test result says. Trust in God, who is the Divine Healer to restore the health of others and yourself!

Scan the QR code to hear Linda Gunter share this story on YouTube!
Episode Title: "Miracles with Mommy Linda-Belinda's Brain"

Susie's Lupus

The name of the individual mentioned in this story has been changed for privacy.

I live on a lake with my beautiful family, and one of our close friends owns a jet ski. One day, this family friend allowed us to borrow her jet ski for an event we were hosting at our home. I was able to drive our guests around on the lake with the jet ski, and we had a lot of fun! One of the guests that I drove around that day was a woman named "Susie". As she rode along with me, we were able to have a conversation despite the loud hum of the jet ski. She explained to me that she and her husband had just recently moved to the area. She shared that they were looking for a church to attend, and she continued to share a few other details of her life with me. It is a very rare occurrence to find me quiet. However, I felt the hair on the back of my neck stand up, and I knew I needed to remain quiet and listen to Susie. We continued to drive around the lake on the jet ski, and I ended the ride knowing a little more about my new friend.

~

After this interaction with Susie, I would see her and her husband when they would come to my house for Bible study group, but shortly after that, it was as if she disappeared! I wouldn't see her around anymore, and I genuinely started to worry about her. I called and sent several texts to Susie, but she would not respond. One thing about me is, if I don't get a response from those I care about, I'm showing up at their house! So that is exactly what I did! I walked up to Susie's house and knocked on the door. Susie answered and invited me in. I was quick to speak and asked Susie if I had done anything wrong or offended her in any way. I explained that everyone in our Bible study group missed her and her family, and I just wanted to know what was keeping them from coming back.

Susie began to share many things with me, and she happened to mention that she had Lupus. We continued to talk about other challenges she was facing, and in the middle of our in-depth conversation, I asked Susie if we could stop and pray specifically for the Lupus that was affecting her body. She agreed, and as we were praying, I felt the Holy Spirit whisper to me that I needed to pray about the self-hatred Susie had about herself. This wasn't something she had brought up to me in our conversations, but I was obedient to the Holy Spirit. I prayed for Susie to surrender the hate she had towards herself. After we finished praying and talking with each other, I went on my way. Susie and her husband never returned to Bible study or any other Love Him Love Them events, but I would pray for them often.

After not hearing from Susie for quite some time, I received a text from her. It stated, "Linda, I don't think I ever shared with you, but the Lord *healed me* of Lupus. It was quite a while ago, and I knew I was healed when you spoke that word of truth to me about the spirit of self-hatred I had in me. I am so thankful for you, and God has put it on my heart to tell you that a *miracle* was done in me. I love you. Thank you Jesus!" It made my heart so happy to know the Lord allowed me to be an instrument in His healing of Susie's Lupus.

My prayer for you is that you will be obedient to the Holy Spirit if He prompts you to say something very specific. It may not make any sense to you, but it's not about you. It is all about allowing His will to be done. If He tells you to pray about something very specific, do it! He placed it on your mind for a reason. When the Lord put that very specific word about self-hatred in my mind, I knew I had to speak out that truth to Susie. It was *exactly* what she needed to hear, and she received a miracle that day! Praise God!

Scan the QR code to hear Linda Gunter share this story on YouTube!
Episode Title: "Miracles with Mommy Linda-Susie's Lupus"

A Healed Heart

One of my closest friends, Shirley, sent a text to our Bible study group. The text mentioned that she was having trouble with her heart, and she was in need of a cardiac catheterization. Shirley was experiencing the intense feeling of her heart racing on a regular basis, and she knew this could be a serious issue. When I received this message, I was on my way home from Atlanta. After reading the news, I knew I needed to see Shirley as soon as I could get to her. I called my husband to let him know I would be home later than anticipated, and I began to drive off to Shirley's home.

When I arrived at Shirley's house, it was pretty late in the evening. She invited me in and explained that her husband was out of town, but she had a close friend staying with her to help walk her through her recent prognosis. We all sat down together, and Shirley continued to explain that she had issues with her knee and eye, but the doctors were mostly concerned for her heart. At that moment, I thought back to a time the Lord healed another friend of mine, Kelly, who was experiencing similar issues with her heart. This encounter with Kelly was the very first miracle of healing I had ever experienced. As I prayed over Kelly's heart, I could feel her heart rate slow down with my own hand. That miraculous moment built my faith and gave me the confidence to pray for the healing of many others, so I was confident the Lord could heal Shirley's heart too. It's a funny way to think about it, but God specializes in changing hearts! He wants to change our lives and live in our hearts, so He is in the heart-healing business! That night, I anointed Shirley with oil and prayed for the healing of her heart.

A few days later, Shirley went through with the heart cath, but after the procedure, she was still having some trouble. The doctors were unsure of what was causing the racing in Shirley's heart, and there was further discussion on how to continue in treating her. The following Sunday, Shirley came to Bible study at my house. As we passed each other at my kitchen island, she said "Linda, I can feel my heart fluttering." At that moment, Shirley had a drink in her hand, and I had some type of snack in mine, but I stopped right there in my kitchen, people all around us, and I prayed again for the Lord to heal Shirley's heart.

Three days after I prayed for Shirley in my kitchen, I received a text in the Bible study group chat. Shirley was so excited to tell us that after going back to the doctor, there were no signs of any heart problems, and the doctor wasn't even going to place her on any type of medication for her heart! Her heart was functioning normally again! What a miracle! Shirley was able to get the cataract surgery she needed in her eye, which she wouldn't have been able to receive if she was experiencing heart problems. Her cardiologist was so excited to see such a miracle unfold before him, and I am sure the Lord used Shirley's healing to speak truth to him.

Is there someone in your life who has asked for prayers of healing? If so, I beg you not to just say, "I will keep you in my prayers." Do you know how many times we say that in passing, but we never actively pray for healing? If someone asks you for a specific prayer, I encourage you to pray as soon as the request is given. Even if you are in a room surrounded with others, be quick to pray confidently for the healing of others!

Pictured: Linda smiles with Shirley at a Bible study gathering.

Scan the QR code to hear Linda Gunter share this story on YouTube!
Episode Title: "The Doctors were Amazed After Heart Issues Healed!"

Maria's Baby

Some of you may know that I am a member of the "Prayerprenuers" clubhouse group. This group joins together on a weekly basis to lift up one another in prayer. During one of our weekly meetings, a lady named "Maria" came into the clubhouse chat, and she had a very specific prayer request for us. Maria and her husband had been trying to get pregnant for the past three years! They desperately wanted a child, and this couple had taken several steps to help with infertility. Of course, I was incredibly eager to pray for Maria because I had prayed for several women going through seasons of infertility, and God blessed those women with children! I had no doubt in my mind that the Lord could do the same for Maria.

After I prayed for Maria, I could tell by her tone of voice that she was a little skeptical of my prayer for healing. I asked Maria if she would be willing to have a conversation over the phone with my daughter, Jeanna. Love Him Love Them has a 24-hour prayer team, and Jeanna is in charge of this prayer group. I knew if Maria could get in touch with Jeanna, the entire prayer group would come together and pray for Maria around the clock. Thankfully, Maria made the call to my daughter, and Jeanna was able to counsel and pray over Maria again.

Three weeks later, I got a phone call from Maria. She said, "Linda, I am pregnant!" I responded with, "Of course you are! That's what we prayed for!" Maria continued to explain to me that for the past three years, she had documented every single menstrual cycle, diet change, and anything else that could possibly be documented to help her conceive. During the meeting through the clubhouse group three weeks prior, Maria heard me talking about the need to surrender all of our needs, wants, and desires to the Lord. She said that I mentioned the importance of giving up control of our lives and giving control to Jesus. Maria realized she was not giving God any opportunity to have a role in her becoming a mother. She said, "That day, you told me to submit and give *everything* to God, and that is exactly what I did. I didn't document anything at all. I just trusted God."

When I remember Maria, I like to think that her story had two miracles. The first miracle is that she and her husband were able to have a child! The second miracle I see is that Maria is now living a righteous life, completely surrendered to God as she trusts Him with her life. I pray you will live a life similar to Maria's. I encourage you to surrender your hurt, unforgiveness, needs, and desires to God. Once you make room for Him in your life, I can assure that you will see Him work in miraculous ways!

Scan the QR code to hear Linda Gunter share this story on YouTube!
Episode Title: "Miracles with Mommy Linda-Maria's Baby"

Jane's Infection

As I was scrolling through social media one day, I came across a post from my friend, Jane. The post read, "Well, this is not quite the scene we had planned for the weekend, but we are here. After receiving treatment last week, I have been sick. What we thought may have been a stomach bug has now turned into a week-long sickness of running to the bathroom, staying in bed, and having the inability to keep any food down." The post continued to explain that Jane decided to go to the emergency room to figure out why she was so sick. After spending five hours in the waiting room, she was moved up to a room. While waiting for test results, Jane was admitted to the oncology department at the hospital in order to receive the fluids her body so desperately needed. Her husband remained by her side throughout the whole ordeal, and they were both ready to have some answers. Jane's post ended by saying,

"What I need right now is prayers for healing, inside and out, and prayers for rest."

Immediately after reading this social media post, I fell to my knees and called my dear friend. She quickly answered the phone, but she asked me to wait for a moment because the doctor was administering medicine to her right as I called. Once she returned back to the phone, I said, "Jane! What in the world is going on!?" She explained to me that she was still unable to keep any food down, and she was experiencing many stomach related issues. She continued to explain her symptoms to me and mentioned that the doctors believed she may have had C. Diff Colitis.

After talking with Jane about her sickness, Psalms 107:20 came to my mind, which says *"He sent out his word and healed them; he rescued them from the grave."* As I prayed, I asked the Lord to send forth healing to Jane's body, and I asked this in complete confidence that the Lord would answer my prayer. Jane and I prayed and talked with each other for about two minutes before another doctor came into the room. Jane had to quickly hang up, but she assured me that she would keep me updated.

Within the next two hours of the phone call with Jane, I received another call from her. She told me that she had just eaten a meal and enjoyed an ICEE drink. As of that phone call, she had not vomited or had to rush to the restroom. I rejoiced with her, and I told her I would continue to keep her in my prayers. About two hours after the second conversation with Jane, she called me again. She said, "I don't have C.Diff. The doctors are changing the steroid I am taking, and I will be heading home soon!" I was so happy to hear this wonderful news, and I thanked God for answering my prayer for healing over Jane.

If you are reading this, I am sure either you or someone you know are experiencing some type of sickness. I encourage you to have the confidence to come before God and ask for healing. Please do not allow Satan to infiltrate your mind with disbelief. God wants to heal his children. Ask Him, in faith, to do what He does best, and I can assure you, a miracle will take place!

Scan the QR code to hear Linda Gunter share this story on YouTube!
Episode Title: "Miracles with Mommy Linda- Jane's Infection"

Pink Eye Healed

My mother is eighty-five years old, and she lives with me. I am so thankful to have the help of my husband and children in taking care of her. I was out at lunch with my friend, Susan, when I received a text from my daughter, Jeanna. In the text was a picture of my mom's eye. It looked as if it were about to explode! Her eye was very red and puffy. It looked awfully painful! I showed the picture to Susan, and she said, "Oh my goodness! Linda, that is pink eye! You need to take her to the doctor before everyone in your house gets it!" I quickly finished my meal and rushed to the car to get to my mom. As I drove home, I called different doctors in the area to try to get her in for an appointment, but each doctor was completely booked for the day. Finally, I decided to call my mom's primary care doctor, whose practice was an hour away from my house! Thankfully, he was able to fit her in, but I had to rush to pick my mom up and get her to the doctor's office before it closed.

When I arrived home, I found my mom on the couch rubbing her eye. After she rubbed her watery and red eye, she went to touch the couch and other items. Of course, I thought we were all going to die of pink eye because my mother was spreading her nasty germs everywhere! I told her, "Stop touching your eye. Pink eye is contagious, and we don't need you spreading it everywhere!" Of course, my mom did not listen to me, and she continued to rub her eye as we headed to the car. As we drove to Athens, it seemed as if my mom's eye was getting worse. It looked more swollen than when I first saw it in Jeanna's picture. It was then that I knew I needed to anoint her with oil and pray for healing over her eye. Unfortunately, I had recently switched purses, and I forgot to place my anointing oil in my new purse. I said, "That's okay! I can still pray, even without my oil!" With one hand on the steering wheel and the other on my mom, I asked the Lord to completely heal her eye.

After I prayed, we continued to drive twenty more minutes to the doctor's office. When we arrived and entered the waiting room, there were sick people everywhere! My close friends and family know that I hate doctors' offices. Needless to say, I don't do well with germs and small spaces! Thankfully, a nurse quickly came to take my mother and I back to a room. The nurse weighed my mom and recorded some vitals. After she finished, she asked us to wait for the doctor to come.

After waiting for some time, the doctor entered the room. As soon as he walked in, I was sure he was Haitian. I was quick to ask him, "Are you from Haiti?" He explained to me that he was actually from Ghana, which is located in

West Africa. I began to share Love Him Love Them's story with him. I said, "We have a hospital in Haiti, and it would be an honor to have you visit!" He responded, "I am not going to Haiti with you now." He had been watching the news of the civil unrest and violence that had been unfolding in Haiti, and he understood the dangers of visiting the country.

After we talked about the ministry, he asked, "Why are the two of you here today?" I pointed to my mom, who was sitting beside me. I said, "I am pretty sure she has pink eye. Her eye is very red and swollen, as you can see." The doctor looked at my mom and then back at me. With a confused tone he asked, "Which eye are you talking about?" Shocked by his response, I looked over at my mom to see that her eye was completely fine! The redness and puffiness was completely gone! Quickly, I pulled out my phone to show the doctor the picture of my mom's eye that was taken a couple hours prior to our visit. When he saw the picture, he said, "Oh wow! That is really really bad!" I said, "I know! That's why I drove an hour here to have her seen!"

The doctor went on to ask me if I had given my mom any medicine to help with the redness and swelling. I told him I had not, but I called Jeanna to see if she had given my mom anything before I picked her up. Jeanna explained that she had given my mom eye drops. The doctor asked Jeanna to text over a picture of the eye drops she used. When he saw the eye drops, he said, "Oh, those eye drops couldn't have fixed the problem she had in her eye." Then, I shared with the doctor that I had prayed in the car for the complete healing of my mother's eye. He said, "Oh! Of course! That explains everything! I had a praying mother, and she always prayed for me when I was sick in Africa. The Lord healed me many times, and I know he healed your mom as well!" He assured me that my mom would be just fine, and she would not need any additional treatment.

Many believe God can heal the big ailments, such as tumors and cancer. However, we often feel silly asking him to heal the little things, such as pink eye. Whether it's a cut on the finger, stage four cancer, or an infection of the eye, you can ask your Heavenly Father for healing! God cares for your well-being. All you have to do is confidently ask Him to heal you, and because of your faith in Him, you will be healed!

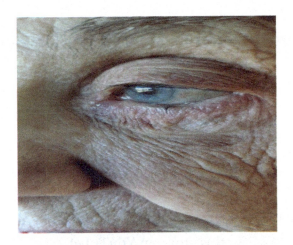

Picture: This is the photo Jeanna sent to Linda.

(From left to right) Ms. Barbara (Linda's mom) smiles for the camera with Linda after the Lord healed her eye!

Scan the QR code to hear Linda Gunter share this story on YouTube!
Episode Title: "God Owes Me Gas Money! I had to Drive an Hour for Him to Heal my Mother's eye"

Chapter Three: Obedience

"Blessed are all who fear the Lord, who walk in obedience to him." -Psalms 128:1

I am a firm believer that a miracle can happen by simply listening to what the Holy Spirit tells us and acting on the things He has told us to do. The world is in desperate need of radical obedience to the Lord's demands. Delayed obedience is just disobedience. I pray this next chapter encourages you to be active in your walk with the Lord. Be quick to listen and obey the things He calls you to do. Even if it may not make sense at the moment, *obey anyway.* Your obedience just may be the answer to someone else's prayer for a miracle!

A Word About Paperwork

During the summer of 2022, my daughter, Jeanna, went on a mission trip to Greece! She had the amazing opportunity to teach English and spread the Gospel to Afghan refugees. During her time in Greece, Jeanna met a woman who was in need of help. The woman needed to complete paperwork that would allow her to remain in the country. This woman had been residing in Greece for the past two years as an Afghan refugee, and she had not heard any news about her refugee status from the embassy or her attorneys. Needless to say, she was worried, and she wanted to ensure she would be able to legally stay in Greece. Jeanna worked with the woman the best she could to help her work through the seemingly never-ending paperwork.

As they worked, Jeanna tried to share the Gospel. Unfortunately, the woman was not interested in hearing about Jesus. Her sole purpose of reaching out to Jeanna was to receive help with paperwork. The woman feared she was in danger of being sent back to Afghanistan, and she was unable to focus on anything besides the paperwork in front of them. Even in her disbelief, the refugee woman allowed Jeanna to pray over her situation as they finished working together. They went their separate ways, but Jeanna continued to keep the woman in her prayers.

At two in the morning the following day, the Holy Spirit woke Jeanna up. He told her to text the Afghan woman she worked with the day before and tell her that she would be informed about her paperwork the very next day. Even in her tiredness and confusion of the Lord's request, Jeanna texted the Afghan woman. However, Jeanna did not text the woman saying *exactly* what the Lord had asked her to say. Jeanna texted, "The Lord woke me up to tell you that you will be hearing about your paperwork soon." As Jeanna laid back down and tried to go to sleep, the Holy Spirit continued to nudge at her heart. She felt as if she didn't fully obey what He asked her to tell the woman. He didn't say that she would hear news about her paperwork soon, He said she would hear about the paperwork *tomorrow*. Jeanna knew if she continued to wrestle in disobedience, she was not going to get any sleep that night! Finally, Jeanna obeyed and texted the woman a second time. She said, "By the way, you will hear about your paperwork tomorrow." After feeling completely satisfied in sharing what the Lord had given her for this refugee woman, Jeanna fell back asleep.

The following day, Jeanna received a shocking text from the woman she messaged the night before. It read, "Girlfriend, you are a powerful prayer warrior! After two years of hearing absolutely nothing, I received a phone call from my attorney this morning, and everything is moving forward with my case!" The woman continued to share that she told her husband about what the Lord told Jeanna the night before. Her husband was also a non-believer, but he was amazed the things Jeanna heard from the Lord came to pass that very day!

Jeanna is now back in the United States. It is unknown if the woman she met and her husband are followers of Christ today, but how exciting is it to know that a beautiful seed was sown into their hearts because of Jeanna's obedience? I believe the Lord built the faith of the sweet couple in Greece, and I know He built Jeanna's as well! I encourage you to not be hesitant to the Lord's instructions. He puts things in our minds for a reason. We *must* be quick to obey for the sake of His kingdom!

Scan the QR code to hear Linda Gunter share this story on YouTube!
Episode Title: "Miracles with Mommy Linda- A Word About Paperwork"

The X-Ray Machine

By the grace of God, Love Him Love Them was able to open a hospital in Haiti during the global COVID-19 pandemic in 2020! We were very blessed to have donor support to help provide much of the medical supplies for the hospital. However, the hospital was still in desperate need of an x-ray machine. This type of medical machine is very difficult to find in the country of Haiti, so I quickly found myself in a rut. The ministry did not have the extra funds at the time to buy an x-ray machine, so we asked people in the community to prayerfully consider being financial sponsors for this need. Weeks went by, and the ministry had not made a dent in providing the funds needed to pay for the x-ray machine, so the idea of obtaining one was placed on the back burner for a while.

~

Due to circumstances out of my control, I had to find a new office space for Love Him Love Them in a very limited time frame. Our previous office space had been sold, and we were needing to be out of the space in two weeks! Of course I received this news inbetween the ministry's two biggest events of the year, Love Him Love Them's Annual Thanksgiving Day Event and The Night of Hope. I had a million other things on my mind, but I frantically made as many calls as I could to find office space for the ministry. After many phone calls, the hospital in my area informed me that they had some extra office space available at an off-campus site. When asked about the ministry's budget for renting office space, I replied, "Well.. I was hoping to get it for free. Love Him Love Them is a non-profit organization, and the money we receive from donors goes to widows and orphans in the country of Haiti and those in need in the

Northeast Georgia area. We do not have the extra funds to pay for office space." Even with my shocking request, I was encouraged to meet with the property owner, and he would consider my appeal.

When I met with the property owner of the new office space, I was blown away! The office was thirty times the size of the office we were previously operating in! It was absolutely beautiful! After I received the grand tour of the space, I had the opportunity to share Love Him Love Them's story with the owner. He was amazed by all of the things the Lord had done in and through the ministry, and he told me, "I think we can give you the space for free." I explained to him that we were in a time crunch and needed to be in the office within a couple of days. He told me that as long as we came in and cleaned up the office, the ministry could have it for free! Oh my goodness! I was so thankful this man was so willing to bless the ministry with an incredible office! As I was thanking him, I heard the Holy Spirit tell me, "Ask him about an x-ray machine." Immediately, I was taken aback. I literally just asked this man for a free office. How in the world could I ask him for a free x-ray machine too?

The Holy Spirit continued to push me to ask the property owner for an x-ray machine. Reluctantly, I asked him, "Would you possibly have access to an x-ray machine?" He replied, "Yes. I know where to get one." Almost embarrassingly, I asked him if I could have it. To my surprise he said, "Actually, I think you would be doing my friend a favor by taking it. It is located in another company office, and that office space has been sold. My friend needs the x-ray machine out of that office." Before I even signed a contract for the office space, I rushed over to the other office where the machine was located. When I arrived, there were contractors in the building making plans to reconstruct the space. I asked the workers to point me in the direction of the x-ray machine. They led me to a dark office filled with construction supplies, but in the back of the room was a beautiful x-ray machine! I called the owner of the space with the x-ray machine to thank him for the generous donation. His response to me was, "Are you kidding me? We have been *praying* that someone would take the x-ray machine out of the office for quite some time. We are so glad you were able to take it off of our hands!"

Not only did Love Him Love Them receive free office space that day, but an x-ray machine was given to us for free! Now, we can continue to serve patients in our hospital in Haiti with the very best medical care and equipment. I thank God for giving me the confidence to ask the property owner for an x-ray machine that day. Even with a reluctant heart, I obeyed the Holy

Spirit, and a need was met for the ministry. Thank you Jesus for this amazing miracle!

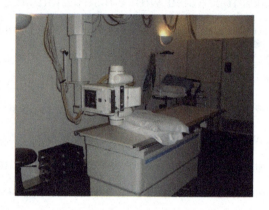

Pictured: The donated x-ray machine to be sent to the Valley of Hope hospital in Haiti

Scan the QR code to hear Linda Gunter share this story on YouTube!
Episode Title: "Miracles with Mommy Linda- The X-Ray Machine"

My Wedding Ring

Before I share this miracle story, I need to give a little preface. Please do not take me as a prideful person when I say that I have an amazingly gorgeous wedding ring. To be fair, I had a starter ring, which is what many women receive from their husbands in their younger years. However, after working through some very difficult challenges in our marriage, my husband and I decided to renew our vows. During the renewal is when I received my new wedding ring that I absolutely adore, and I cherish it even more now because I am reminded of how the Lord helped my husband and I overcome many trials.

~

Love Him Love Them's Haitian Orphan Children's Choir had the opportunity to perform at Mother Emanuel AME Church in Charleston, South Carolina. You may recognize the name of the church because it is the same location where Dylann Roof brutally murdered nine church members in 2015. During our visit at the church, a child from the choir began to experience a demonic manifestation. To rule out medical issues, an ambulance was called. However, I am confident that I witnessed a demonic phenomenon that day. It was very clear to me that Mother Emanuel AME was experiencing spiritual warfare in the strongest sense. Needless to say, this choir visit held quite a bit of chaos!

After the demonic manifestation passed and the ambulance cleared, I was in a hurry to get the children and myself back on the bus to head back home. As I was getting on the bus, my wedding ring snagged my shirt. When I looked down, I noticed the diamond in my ring was gone! Oh my goodness! What else could possibly go wrong at this church? I decided to retrace my steps in the church parking lot. I even opted to go back into the church building to search for the missing diamond there. I crawled around searching for the diamond for what seemed like hours, but I never found it.

A few days after the wedding ring incident, I went to a jewelry store to get an estimated cost for a replacement diamond. The jeweler gave me a ridiculously high price that I was unwilling to pay, so I decided to get a $75 piece of glass! Trust me, you could *never* tell the difference! Shortly after getting the glass replacement, I lost my wedding ring. I could not find it anywhere! Now I know this was not a huge tragedy I was facing. I had lost my wedding ring many times before, and I'm sure many of you reading along have also had this same experience. One time, when I lost my wedding ring prior to this situation, I found it on my daughter's dresser in her room. When I asked Mirlanda why she had it there after I had been searching for quite some time for it, she responded, "Oh, I was saving it. I wanted to give it to you for Mother's Day!" Of course, at that time, Mother's Day was six months away. Needless to say, I got my ring back that day. Because of that incident, I checked with Mirlanda to see if she was "saving" my ring for Christmas or some other holiday, but Mirlanda had no clue where my wedding ring was. I really started to worry. After ten days of searching, I told my husband that I really did believe I had lost the ring for good, and we were both very disappointed.

In my desperation, I almost jokingly prayed, "Lord, where is my wedding ring?" Immediately, the Holy Spirit responded, "Go over to your night stand, and look in the corner next to the box you have placed there." I was very confused by this response because it seemed to be a very random spot for my ring to be, and I had never left it in that particular place before. Even though I didn't fully understand, I was quick to obey. I walked over to the corner and pulled the curtain back to reveal the space next to the box I had in the spot. Do you want to guess what was there? My wedding ring! I picked it up and excitedly told my husband, "David! I asked God where my wedding ring was, and He told me!" Of course he responded, "Well you should have done that a long time ago!"

Can you believe it took me ten days to *finally* ask God for help in finding my wedding ring? Sometimes God uses silly little lessons like losing a wedding ring to teach us how to rely on Him in *every* circumstance. I pray God will be the one you call first in your time of need. I encourage you to make room for Him, even in the small and mundane things of life. When He gives you direction, be quick to obey, even if you don't fully understand.

Scan the QR code to hear Linda Gunter share this story on YouTube!

Episode Title: "Miracles with Mommy Linda- My Wedding Ring"

Update on Jane

To read Jane's original story, please refer to Chapter Two: Miraculous Healings.

After receiving healing from an awful infection, I heard news from Jane's mom that Jane was going to have a biopsy procedure. During a scan, Jane's doctor noticed nodules in her lungs. Her doctor saw fit to schedule a biopsy to ensure the nodules were non-cancerous. Of course, after Jane heard news of the nodules, she informed her family and friends. They joined together in praying for another miracle of healing over Jane's body. They had seen God heal her of a terrible infection weeks before, and they were confident He could heal her again.

A couple of weeks after Jane received her prognosis for the nodules in her lungs, she had to get a CT scan. This was the first step needed to be taken before the biopsy treatment could take place. Jane underwent the CT scan, and what the doctors saw on the scan results shocked them. There were no nodules in her lungs! She had been healed *again*! Praise God!

Jane's second healing reminded me of one of my favorite verses, Psalms 107:20. This verse says, *"He sent forth His word and healed them; He rescued them from the pit."* Jane did not have all of her friends and family members physically pray over her. However, she knew those who loved her would "send forth" healing to her body, just as Jesus did. Because of their obedience in praying for healing, the Lord answered their fervent prayers and healed Jane!

Is your disobedience to God hindering someone else in your life? Has God asked you to pray for someone, maybe someone you aren't too fond of? Has the Lord given you a specific task that you haven't followed through with? I encourage you to not delay in obeying the Father's command. As I have mentioned before, delayed obedience is just disobedience. When you completely surrender to the Lord and obey His commands, miracles can and will happen all around you!

Scan the QR code to hear Linda Gunter share this story on YouTube!
Episode Title: "Miracles with Mommy Linda- Update on Jane"

Chapter Four: Divine Intervention

"Many are the plans in a person's heart, but it is the Lord's purpose that prevails."- Proverbs 19:21

God loves setting up divine appointments for His children! I find so much joy in looking back at the miracles I have experienced and seeing how the Lord orchestrated the circumstances surrounding the miraculous events. Whether it is in the grocery store, carpool, church, or somewhere you never even planned to be, God intervenes in miraculous ways to further His kingdom. As you read this chapter, I encourage you to thank God for the divine interventions He set up for your good and His glory! I highly recommend that you be quick to obey the prompting of the Holy Spirit, even when you do not fully understand! I am convinced this is how divine intervention works. If you want to be used as an instrument for God's supernatural works, you *must* act when He says to!

From Death to Life

My husband, David, and I have the privilege of joining another couple for a double-date night every week. One of our favorite spots is a restaurant that offers free oysters on Wednesday nights. I hate oysters, but the husbands in our group love them, so that restaurant is where we seem to land quite often. On our way to the restaurant one night, we heard a very loud and alarming crash as we turned onto the highway. We all turned and noticed a man on a motorcycle had been hit by a car! My husband is a first responder, so we pulled the car over. As David rushed to the aid of the motorcyclist, I worked with the other couple to help stop traffic across the four- lane highway. We were the very first people on the scene, and it was truly a terrifying moment.

When David reached the man lying on the road, he began to check for signs of life. David asked the man questions to check for consciousness, but he received no response. The motorcyclist still had his helmet on as David checked for a pulse, but he could not find one. The man was dead. At this point, traffic had stopped, and I was kneeled down next to David. When David told me the devastating news, I immediately placed my hands on the man lying dead in front of me, and I began to pray. I had an unexplainable gut feeling that the man was not saved. He was on his way to hell, and he was in desperate need of a second chance. I prayed and pleaded for the Lord to raise this man back to life so he could have the opportunity to accept Jesus as his Lord and Savior.

Towards the beginning of my prayer, David was still checking for signs of life. The motorcyclist still had no pulse, and David insisted that he was dead. I continued to pray over the man. I desperately wanted him to be brought from death to life to hear the good news of Jesus. After about two minutes of praying, the man became conscious! David began to ask him the proper questions first responders should ask, but I quickly interrupted my husband to ask the man if he knew Jesus as his personal Savior. No ambulance or police cars had arrived at this point, but I could hear the sirens. I knew my opportunity to speak to him was very limited. Even in his confusion from the accident, the man told me he was not a follower of Christ. After asking him a few more questions, I began to share the path to salvation with him. Unfortunately, the EMTs arrived before the man was able to accept the invitation to salvation. I was quickly moved aside for the medical personnel to do their work, and the man was put into the ambulance and rushed to the hospital.

To be honest, I was a little disappointed that I was unable to lead the man to the Lord. However, I completely missed the miracle I witnessed right before my very own eyes that night. A dead man was brought back to life! He now had a second chance, and God saw fit for me to plant a seed in his life that night in the middle of the road. Even in the chaos of a tragic accident, the Lord made a divine appointment I absolutely could not miss! I am unsure where the man is today, but I pray the seed that was planted in his heart that night is continuing to be watered. The Lord has an amazing plan for his life. I am sure of it!

Jesus desires for His children to know their Heavenly Father, and He so deeply longs to have a relationship with that man. I encourage you to pray in complete boldness when you ask the Lord for something, even if it seems as crazy as raising someone from the dead! *You* may be the reason for someone's second chance! *You* may be the instrument the Lord wants to use for His plan to salvation. Jesus performs miracles through us every day. Nothing is too far for Him! Trust in that truth today!

Scan the QR code to hear Linda Gunter share this story on YouTube!

Episode Title: "Miracles with Mommy Linda- Dead Man on a Motorcycle"

The Bus

During Love Him Love Them's tour with the Haitian Orphan Children's Choir, a bus was used to transport all thirty Haitian children and their chaperones up and down the east coast. That bus ended up being more trouble than it was worth because we would oftentimes find ourselves on the side of the road due to some kind of mechanical issue. I can't even begin to count how many times the bus needed to be towed as I made arrangements to have transportation for all the children in my care. Even in the frustration, the Lord still found ways to use the choir and myself to witness to those in need. Whether it was a mechanic needing to hear the good news of the Gospel or a Good Samaritan needing some encouragement, God *always* showed up in miraculous ways!

After the choir tour, the bus completely broke down. The transmission and radiator had gone out. The transmission was able to be fixed. However, I could not find a radiator for the bus anywhere! For a year and two months, I could not find a radiator. It was so frustrating to see the bus parked in one spot, completely useless. The bus quickly became a burden to me, and I did not know what to do.

One day, I received a phone call from my dear friend, Jody Bennett. She runs a nonprofit called "Unity on a Mission". During our phone conversation, she said, "Linda, have you ever thought about giving your bus away?" I told her that after all the trouble I had with the bus, I would LOVE to give it away! I wanted it completely off my hands! However, I knew I would feel horrible giving someone a bus that couldn't be driven. How tacky is that!? Jody began to tell me that at one of the events for her ministry, there was a man in attendance who was in need of a bus. This man worked for an organization in Athens, Georgia, and the mission of his organization was to mentor young men. For over a year, he searched for a bus to use to transport the men he was mentoring, but he was unsuccessful.

Jody continued to encourage me to consider giving the bus away to this man and his organization. I told her it felt so wrong to give away something so terribly broken, but then she told me something very surprising. She said, "Did I not tell you? He has the exact same bus as you have. The motor in his bus does not work, but the radiator works just fine. He can take the parts of your bus that work and place them into his bus to get it up and going again!" Apparently, the radiator I had been searching for was no longer being manufactured. This explained why I was having so much trouble finding one! Jody explained that volunteers with the organization would be willing to tow the bus themselves, and they would greatly appreciate the wonderful gift of the bus.

I love thinking back to this miracle because I can see how the Lord orchestrated everything in His perfect timing. What was a burden to me quickly became a blessing to someone else. Who knew that my ministry's run down bus would be the answer to another man's prayer? The Lord knew, and He miraculously intervened to make it happen! What a mighty God we serve!

Scan the QR code to hear Linda Gunter share this story on YouTube!
Episode Title: "Miracles with Mommy Linda- The Bus"

Hit and Run

Certain names of the individuals mentioned in this story have been changed for privacy.

The Lord has truly blessed me with speaking engagements and opportunities to share with others about Love Him Love Them. Most Sundays, I am at a different church to speak about all the amazing things God is doing in and through the ministry. At one of my speaking engagements, I was limited to about ten to twelve minutes of sharing because the pastor still planned to preach after I spoke. I always find it so difficult to explain the story of Love Him Love Them when I am in a time crunch, but I trusted the Lord would speak through me during the service. As I was speaking, about twelve or so people walked in and filled up an entire row. I immediately made eye contact with one of the women coming in with the large group, and I felt the Holy Spirit impress something special on my heart. He made it clear that my sole purpose for visiting the church was to speak with her. A few minutes later, I finished my message and sat down to hear the pastor's sermon and the conclusion of the service. All the while, I was eagerly waiting to speak with the woman a few rows back from me.

After the service, the Lord reminded me of my task. He said, "Go speak to that lady." Of course, I was quick to obey, and I walked up to the woman. When I approached her, I introduced myself and asked her if there was anything I could pray about for her. Before I could get too many words out of my mouth, the woman began to cry, almost uncontrollably. She introduced herself as "Brianna" and asked if we could go into another room for the sake of privacy. We quickly moved to another room so Brianna could freely share her troubles with me. After talking through some challenging life circumstances with her, I asked if she knew Jesus as her Lord and Savior. She told me that she did not. I was so blessed to have the opportunity to lead Brianna to the Lord. After leading her to salvation, it was clear that during our time of prayer together, a demonic spirit had fled from her. She continuously stated, "I feel like something has left me.. something just left me." Of course something left her! When we come to know Jesus as the Lord of our lives, *everything* that is not of Him must flee! I was so excited for Brianna's newly found faith, and I wanted to give her a Bible and a few of the ministry's special products.

Somehow, I got turned around and ended up leaving the church without giving Brianna a Bible. For my close friends and family, it is no surprise to find me forgetful! However, as I was driving back home with my husband, I said, "Oh my goodness! David, I forgot to give that woman a Bible! We have to turn around!"

Thankfully, we hadn't traveled too far down the road, and we quickly turned back towards the church. When I arrived, Brianna was still in the parking lot. Quickly, I got out of the car and rushed over to her to give her a Bible and a *Choir of Angels* book. As I was passing the books over to her, a friend of hers named "Shay" walked up to me and explained that she would love to purchase a book to help support the ministry. Then, Shay asked if I would be willing to pray for her. I responded "Of course! What would you like me to pray for?" She began to explain to me that two years prior, one of her sons was killed in a hit and run accident. Since the tragedy, another one of her sons had become addicted to heroin. She said, "Please pray for my son to be free of this addiction. He's walking the streets, and I have no contact with him." After hearing Shay's story, I prayed over her. I remember asking the Lord to perform a *supernatural intervention* in her son's life so he could be free of his addiction to heroin. After we finished praying and headed our separate ways, I thanked God for putting me in the paths of Brianna and Shay.

The very next day, I received a phone call from Brianna. Thankfully, one of the Haitian girls who attended the speaking engagement with me wrote my phone number in the book for Brianna's convenience. I was surprised when Brianna shared with me that the night before, Shay's son had been hit by a car! I said, "You mean the son we prayed for yesterday afternoon? The one who was addicted to heroin?" She began to tell me that as he was walking on the street, he was hit by a car. It was a hit and run incident. My heart sank, and I was prepared to hear that Shay's son had passed. However, Brianna said, "He's alive! Shay is in the hospital with him now, but his legs are not working."

I remember thinking back to the prayer I said the day before. I asked for a supernatural intervention, not a hit and run! Before hanging up the phone, Brianna asked me to visit Shay and her son in the hospital as soon as I had the chance. I asked Brianna to have Shay call me because I didn't want to show up unannounced and uninvited. To my surprise, Shay called me two minutes after I spoke with Brianna. She said, "Linda, do you remember what you prayed yesterday? A supernatural intervention just took place! My son can't walk. He can't walk out of the hospital to get drugs!" It seemed almost strange to have any amount of joy after such a tragic accident, but I understood Shay's mentality. The Lord gave her son a second chance. He did not have the option to run from his problems. He had to face them under the professional care of a team of doctors and alongside a praying mother. Shay's son was able to detox in the hospital as he received medical attention for the injuries he received from the accident. As he healed, Shay stayed with him and read *Choir of Angels*, a book filled with miraculous accounts! I had the privilege of visiting Shay and her son in the hospital, and I prayed over the two of them. Their story became such a testimony to the doctors and nurses in the hospital, all because of the Lord performing a supernatural intervention!

Pictured: Linda stands with Brianna after she accepted Jesus as her Lord and Savior!

Scan the QR code to hear Linda Gunter share this story on YouTube!

Episode Title: "Miracles with Mommy Linda- Hit and Run"

Raped at Sixteen

The names of the individuals mentioned in this story have been changed for privacy.

I am a part of a clubhouse group online called "Prayerprenuers". It is set up to be a tool for entrepreneurs to join together for prayer on a weekly basis. There are people from all over the world in this clubhouse group, and it is very common to witness miracles unfold right before one's eyes during our clubhouse prayer times. Interestingly enough, the tagline for this group states, "Come expecting miracles."

One day, I was in the Prayerprenuers clubhouse room, and I was talking with people and praying as requests came up in the chat. Somehow, there is a back channel in this clubhouse room, and there are people in the group that help moderate this back channel for me. None of that back channel stuff makes any sense to me! Anyways, I had a member from the group message me privately stating that there was a woman in the back channel claiming to be suicidal and was planning to kill her five-year-old daughter. In complete shock and disbelief that someone could so willingly admit to something so heinous, I said, "Well, help me switch things over to this channel so that I can speak with her."

Quickly, a woman named "Abby" came up on my screen. I remember her being very melancholy. The first thing she said to me was, "I am not suicidal. I *am* going to kill myself, and I have decided that I am also going to kill my daughter. I will kill her first, and then I will kill myself." I asked her if we could talk things through, and thankfully, she agreed. It was very clear to me that this woman was from another country. I believe she was from Nigeria. Since Love Him Love Them works so closely with

Haiti, I understand the devastation and hopelessness that is often found among those who live in third world countries, so I found it easy in the moment to empathize with this hurting woman.

Abby went on to tell me that she had been attempting to obtain a F-1 student visa to come to America. Ironically enough, I understood the difficult process of obtaining this type of visa because my husband and I had to go through it with our Haitian children. She explained to me that one of the requirements needed through the embassy was to prove she had financial wherewithal to come to The United States. Amazingly, Abby had already obtained a degree in pharmacy in her country, and she was wanting to come to the States to get her master's degree. Abby went on to say that her mother had been helping her throughout the entire application process for the student visa. However, her mother "slumped" in January. I was taken aback by the wording she used, and I asked her to explain what "slumped" meant. She then told me, "She slumped over and died. I was going to leave my five-year-old daughter with my mother when I went to the States, but now, that is no longer an option." Abby continued by saying that she was unable to find a job in her country. She had an abundance of knowledge and skills to use in a workplace, but she was unable to find any work. On top of all of this, Abby and her daughter no longer had a home. They were unable to stay in the home they shared with Abby's mother. Therefore, since she had no home, and no means to work to provide for herself or her child, the only option besides starving to death would be to kill her daughter and herself.

After listening to Abby's story, I asked her if she had ever prayed about this situation, and I also asked if she had a personal relationship with Jesus Christ. After I asked her those questions, something in me prompted me to ask her if there was anyone in her life who she needed to forgive. She quickly spat back at me in a bitter tone and told me she had been raped at the age of sixteen, and her daughter was the by-product of this rape. Abby began ranting to me about how she had already forgiven the man who raped her, but it was very clear to me by the anger in her voice that this was not true.

Unbeknownst to me, there was another lady in the clubhouse room named Whitney, and she popped in the room right before Abby began to tell her story. Whitney interrupted me and said, "Linda, I was raped when I was sixteen. I have a daughter. I tried to kill my daughter and myself. I want to speak *truth* and *life* over Abby." With tears streaming down my face I asked God, "How did you orchestrate this divine appointment?" Whitney went on to tell me that she had not initially planned to come into the clubhouse room that morning, but she felt led by the Holy Spirit to be there. Whitney was quick to obey, even when she did not fully understand.

Whitney was able to talk Abby off the ledge because she had walked through the very same darkness all those years ago. Whitney started a GoFund me account, and over the course of two days, Whitney's family and friends raised $10,000 for Abby, and they committed to help her obtain her F-1 student visa. A school program was found for Abby in America, and she was able to bring along her daughter! God saw fit to intervene in Abby's life by providing a wonderful friend for her through Whitney. I pray that *you* will be a Whitney to an Abby in your life. Stand firm in your confidence in the Lord, and speak truth and life to those who need it the most.

Scan the QR code to hear Linda Gunter share this story on YouTube!

Episode Title: "Miracles with Mommy Linda- Raped at 16"

Chapter Five: Spiritual Warfare

"For our struggle is not against flesh and blood, but against the rulers, against the authorities, against the powers of this dark world and against the spiritual forces of evil in the heavenly realms." -Ephesians 6:12

Angels, demons, and spiritual warfare exist today, but because of God's protection, you do not have to live in fear of the supernatural. God has given you the powerful weapon of His Word to use against demonic forces. The Bible reminds us of God's power and what is true. Through the Word of God, you can see that you have been given "..authority to tread on serpents and scorpions, and over all the power of the enemy, and nothing shall hurt you." In this chapter, you will read accounts of the supernatural and demonic forces. Because of the Lord's omnipotent power, miracles were performed in the lives of those in desperate need of Christ's intervention. The Lord has equipped you to live free from the bondage of spiritual warfare. Trust in His protection and faithfulness!

Josey's Attitude Adjustment

The name of the individual mentioned in this story has been changed for privacy.

I host a Bible study group in my home every Sunday night. Every week, we join together for a meal and time for fellowship, and then we study the Word of God together. During a busy week of travel for me, I received a text from my daughter, Jeanna, which read, "I know a married couple who would love to come to Bible study on Sunday. They have been having a lot of problems with their teenage daughter. She is rebellious and has an awful attitude. This couple would love to have some support." I asked Jeanna to give the couple my phone number in hopes that they would reach out to me and get connected with the Bible study group.

During the few days I was out of town, I waited to hear from the couple, but I never did. With the chaos of traveling, I forgot they were planning to come to Bible study on the same Sunday I would be returning home. As I pulled up to my house after a long trip out of town, I saw several familiar cars, and I knew the Bible study group had already arrived. It was so nice to come home to my family and sweet friends! As I walked in the door, I noticed a family of five that I had never met before eating dinner with the rest of the group. It did not register in my mind that this new family was the couple Jeanna spoke to me about with their three children. I introduced myself, and I quickly noticed the teenager in the family, Josey. She did not seem like she wanted to be at Bible study. It was then that I realized this was the family in need of support because of Josey's behavior.

After dinner, the group headed downstairs to start our study. For some reason, I felt impressed by the Holy Spirit to invite Josey to sit next to me. My invitation seemed to lighten her mood a bit, and she willingly sat next to me. Throughout the night, I would joke back and forth with Josey and pass silly notes to her. At one point, Josey drew a picture for me to keep. Overall, we had a fun time together! After Bible study, I told Josey and her family goodbye, and I looked forward to getting to know them more.

The next day, I received a text from Josey's mother. It read, "I don't know what happened last night, but Josey has been a completely different girl today. Her attitude is completely different! I've thanked Jesus all day, and I have been praying." As a mother myself, I understood the joy Josey's mother had. We love to see our children thrive! After I spoke with Josey's mom, I remembered back to when my friends and family helped me stake the property around my home with tent posts that had scriptures written on them. I wanted my home to be completely protected from the attacks of Satan, and I knew the Word of God would be the best weapon I could ever have! We prayed a very specific prayer as we staked the four corners of my property. We prayed, "Lord, if anyone enters this home dealing with any type of spiritual warfare or demonic forces, we ask that those struggles would immediately bow down to God and disappear completely!" After receiving the text about Josey's better attitude, I knew it was because of the faith my family and friends had in God to protect those entering my home!

Many times in the Bible, more than prayer is needed to see a miracle unfold. Some accounts in the Bible speak of prayer *and* fasting. Others speak of prayer *and* the anointing with oil. Sometimes you need an *act of faith* along with your prayers! When we took the act of faith in staking the property, a supernatural fence of protection was created, and anything that was not of God had to flee! Now, if a demon possessed individual comes into my home, one of two things can happen. That individual will not be allowed in the home at all due to the supernatural protection of God, or that person will undergo powerful conviction. I truly believe Josey experienced a conviction in her heart during Bible study. Even as we joked and passed notes to each other, Josey had the opportunity to hear the Word of God and truth. I remembered the message my husband gave to the group during Bible study the night before. He emphasized the importance of listening to the Shepherd's voice instead of the voices of Satan. My prayer for Josey is that she will continue to listen to the voice of God and allow His instruction to guide her life.

If you are a parent with a child like Josey, I encourage you to surround your family with a Christ-centered community. Find a church or Bible study group that is willing to lift your family up in prayer and support you through challenging times. Finally, do you need to take an act of faith to help restore your family and home? Whether that action is staking your home with tent posts filled with scriptures or praying over the room of your troubled teenager, I ask you to pair your prayers with a powerful action of faith. I can assure you will see demonic forces flee and prayers answered!

Scan the QR code to hear Linda Gunter share this story on YouTube!
Episode Title: "Miracles with Mommy Linda- Josey's Attitude Adjustment"

Baptized by the Holy Spirit

During the first tour with Love Him Love Them's Haitian Orphan Children's Choir, many of the children experienced intense spiritual warfare. After witnessing a few demonic manifestations amongst a handful of children, I decided to try to find help in learning how to pray and cast out demons in the midst of spiritual warfare. Unfortunately, many of the children in the choir were raised in environments that were infiltrated with voodoo practices. Therefore, demonic activity was present amongst many of them.

How was I supposed to just reach out to someone for help in casting out demons? That's a pretty tough request for most people. Instead, I decided to use Google and research the topic myself. I ended up in a rabbit hole on the internet, and I did not find any helpful information. I knew I needed to find someone willing to help me! I reached out to local friends and family members, but I couldn't find anyone with the information I needed.

Finally, I came upon a very stylish woman in her nineties named "Marilyn Hickey". My close friends and family know I love fashion, and I loved how this woman matched her clothes, jewelry, and shoes! Even more intriguing than her sense of style were her sermons! I quickly became a fan of her work, and I loved her Bible-centered teaching. Marilyn Hickey had a sermon titled, "The Baptism of the Holy Spirit", and the message positively impacted my life. She explained the difference between salvation and the baptism of the Holy Spirit in a way that I could really grasp and understand.

After I listened to Marilyn's message, I called the most Godly man I knew, Pastor Maxeau, our man on the ground in the country of Haiti. Hoping for an answer to the troubles I had been having with some of the choir children, I asked Pastor Maxeau, "Have you ever been baptized in the Holy Spirit?" Laughingly, Maxeau responded, "Oh, Linda! Of course I have!" Then, I asked, "Will you please tell me how I can do that?" Maxeau proceeded to pray for me all the way from Haiti. He asked the Holy Spirit to completely baptize me. In the same way I asked Jesus to be the Lord of my life, I made the decision to believe in the Holy Spirit's ability to do greater works in me.

One week later, a friend of mine did not attend our weekly Bible study group in my home because of a terrible tooth abscess. The entire group gathered after Bible study and called her to pray for healing over her tooth. When she first answered, she was in terrible pain, and the tooth had become horribly infected. I remembered the decision I made to be baptized in the Holy Spirit, and I knew I could confidently come before the Lord and ask for healing over my friend's tooth. After we prayed together, my friend felt absolutely no pain in her tooth! The swelling went down, and it was as if she never had an abscess!

After the prayer, another member of the Bible study group, Kelly, asked for prayer over a heart arrhythmia. Kelly had been to several doctors and tried several different medications, but her heart continued to beat at an abnormally fast rate. In confidence, I placed my hand on Kelly's heart and asked the Lord to completely heal her. As I prayed, I could physically feel Kelly's heart beat slow down. That moment completely blew my mind! To see a miracle performed right in front of my eyes built my faith in an unexplainable way. Since that night, I have seens dozens of miracles unfold!

I stand today as a *true* believer of the supernatural power of the Holy Spirit. When I was baptized through Him, I began to truly place my faith in what the Bible says. Because I am full of the Holy Spirit, He can't help but flow through me! I firmly believe the same can happen for you. You can combat spiritual warfare through the power of the Holy Spirit, and you can make the decision today to ask Him to do greater works in and through you!

(From left to right) Pastor Maxeau, the man who counseled Linda about the baptism of the Holy Spirit, waits for a flight at the airport with David and Linda Gunter.

Scan the QR code to hear Linda Gunter share this story on YouTube!

Episode Title: "Miracles with Mommy Linda-Baptized by the Holy Spirit"

A Note to Readers

The next three miracle stories are excerpts from Linda Gunter's *Choir of Angels: How 30 Orphans Changed Their World*. If these stories of spiritual warfare and the supernatural power of God help build your faith, please consider purchasing a copy of *Choir of Angels*. Scan the QR code below to purchase today!

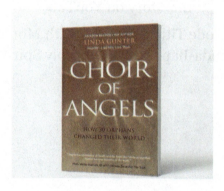

Jeremy's Story (Part One)

Excerpted from Linda Gunter's Choir of Angels:How 30 Orphans Changed Their World

One evening, I had the rare opportunity to have a conversation with just the musicians. None of the children from the choir were around. We were talking about many different things that had happened during the choir tour, and we spoke about their future and the possibility of attending college, a dream all the boys wanted to make a reality. At one point in the conversation, the topic of the three choir girls who were often involved in the demonic manifestations came up. Mostly, the guys were looking for some sympathy given how late they'd had to stay up in order to control whichever one of the three girls was having a manifestation on any given night. They were understandably tired, and they were complaining, in a nice way, about having to help. I apologized to them and told them how grateful I was for all their help.

One of the musicians, the biological son of the man and woman who ran the LifeSaver orphanage in Haiti, spoke up. Having lived with all the girls for years, he said, "Mommy Linda, two of them actually have an uncle who is a head voodoo priest. His name is Jeremy. We have seen him before. He is crazy! We all think that Jeremy has placed voodoo curses on those girls."

Not believing what I was hearing, I asked, "What? Are you serious? No. That doesn't even make sense. Why in the world would anyone do that?" And then, for the first time throughout all the madness, I heard the most logical explanation ever. "Because, Mommy Linda, the voodoo people are very jealous. They are jealous that we all got to come to the United States from Haiti, and they did not." He continued, "They are even more upset because the reason we are here is to sing about Jesus and to share the Gospel." I was in shock but intently listening. I sat quietly digesting what this young man was saying. It certainly made sense. It was crazy, but it made sense. Thinking through every incident that had occurred, it really made me angry, but it made sense. Then, he kept talking. "Some people came to the orphanage before we left for America for this year's choir tour and told us they had learned something new." Not fully understanding what he meant, I asked, "What do you mean something new?" He replied, "They said the voodoo people in Haiti now know how to astral-project, and they were very proud that they would be able to visit the children spiritually and cast spells on us while we were in the United States."

The first time I witnessed the demonic attack with Michelin, I reacted with disbelief and fear. Not knowing what to believe and whether or not to trust what I had seen and heard, I watched and prayed. When the first attack turned into a second, and the second turned into a third, my weary spirit was ready to call in the experts to bring it all to an end. After repeatedly being told it wouldn't happen again, followed by yet another incident, I was desperate for answers. I was in the middle of a major spiritual battle between heaven and the demonic realm! I had my closet community fasting, praying, and seeking God for help with this nightmare! I turned to scripture, absorbing every resource available to me on the spiritual realm. I was ready to brandish the sword of truth and fight in the spiritual realm through the Holy Spirit's power in me. I fought hard with prayer and truth, but as the attacks continued without reprieve, I grew tired. It became increasingly tempting to shut down the tour and just send the kids home. Members of our core Bible study group fasted and prayed. Our Board of Directors were on 24-hour prayer vigils. We searched the Word and sought counsel. This was not just me looking for answers. Many others were closely involved. Throughout our choir tour, I knew I had a daily choice to make. I could continue down the path of fear, frustration, and perceived failure, or I could fight. With the first big puzzle piece in hand, that day I was ready to fight.

Ready to jump on a plane and confront the problem head on through whatever means necessary, I asked, "Where is this voodoo priest, Jeremy?" The response I received was, "Oh, I don't know. I've only seen him a couple of times and from a distance. Everyone is scared of him. He is very powerful." The other musicians began chiming in because they had also heard of Jeremy. "What do I have to do to meet him?", I asked. After a pause, all of them started laughing hysterically. "Oh, Mommy Linda, that would never happen! Even if it could happen, that would be a horrible idea, and we would never let you meet him. It would be too dangerous." I walked away from our conversation with a firm conviction on my mind and in my heart. Challenge accepted. Little did I know the battle had just begun!

Kenol and Lisa

*Excerpted from Linda Gunter's *Choir of Angels: How 30 Orphans Changed Their World**

I remembered my conversation with the musicians as they told me about the girls' uncle, Jeremy, and his involvement in voodoo. I decided at that moment on the plane that I was going to set up a meeting with this voodoo priest when I got to Haiti. To be brutally honest, my initial thoughts were centered around the idea of killing him. I wanted to hurt him, punish him, and yell at him. I really wanted to find some way to hurt him for all the trouble, fiascos, grief, sleepless nights, and pain he had caused me, many other people, and especially the girls. My only problem was I couldn't figure out how I was going to find him in Haiti. At that very moment, I heard God speak very clearly to me. "Linda, you will find Jeremy and you will meet with him, but you are not going to kill him. You are going to lead him to me." I spoke out loud, "No, I am not!" When I realized I was speaking out loud, I opened my eyes. I said again under my breath, "Lord, there is no way I'm telling him about you. I only want to hurt him the same way he has hurt us for the past two years." Apparently, the conversation was over because I didn't hear anything else. I slept the rest of the flight. We landed safely in Haiti. I parted ways with the children at the airport, but not before making arrangements to go to the beach the next day for a big celebration. I went to spend the night at the guesthouse, and the children all returned to the orphanage.

The next morning, I arrived at the orphanage in the huge cattle truck, which was the only transportation we had that could hold all of us. We were prepared for a wonderful day at the beautiful beach in Haiti. As all of the children were piling into the truck, I pulled Paul William, the director of the orphanage, to the side. I told him I wanted him to contact the girls' Uncle Jeremy and have him meet me at the orphanage when I returned from the beach with the kids later that night. His eyes almost popped out of his head. He asked, "Jeremy? Jeremy, who?" I said, "Jeremy, the voodoo priest." Startled, he looked at me as if I was a ghost and said, "How do you know about Jeremy?" I explained to him, "Your sons told me the whole story. I want to meet him." Paul responded, "There is no way for me to contact him, Mommy Linda, and even if I could find him, he cannot come to the orphanage. He is very dangerous and a very powerful, evil man. I cannot help you with this request." I looked back at Paul William as seriously and as intently as I knew how and said, "He needs to be here when we return from the beach today." Many of the nosy and curious children overheard my conversation. I jumped up into the cattle truck with all the kids to leave.

~

As we pulled into the orphanage, I started hearing, "Look, Mommy Linda, the voodoo people are here!" I didn't really pay attention at first. Now all of the children were saying and almost singing, "Mommy Linda, the voodoo people are here!" I was focused on making sure everyone was getting their belongings off the truck. It had been a long day, and all the kids were finally ready to run inside and go straight to bed. I went inside the orphanage to tuck the children in and say good night. Paul William met me at the bottom of the steps. He said, "Okay, Mommy Linda, I did the best I could to meet your request. Jeremy's daughter is here." I was so tired, I started to form the words on my lips to ask who Jeremy was and why his daughter was there. All at once the pieces of the puzzle came together in my mind. I had completely forgotten my demand that morning to have the voodoo priest, Jeremy, at the orphanage upon our return from the beach. Paul William waved his hands directing me to go up the stairs to where the voodoo people were.

As I began walking up the stairs, Pastor Maxeau came into the orphanage from the cattle truck to get me. He wanted to know what was stalling me. He reminded me we still had another 90-minute drive, and that it was not a good idea for a "blanco" (a white person) to be out on the streets in Haiti after dark. I motioned for him to follow me up the steps. During the trip up the 15 steps, I explained to Maxeau my plan to kill, hurt, and punish the people who had caused all the struggles we had on the choir tours with the girls. He followed me, listening intently.

Arriving at the top of the stairs, I looked to my right and saw what looked like a 20-year-old lady and a young man in his early 30s. They looked like Haitian Ken and Barbie dolls. He was very clean cut and handsome, and she was absolutely gorgeous. Paul William introduced us to this young couple, and he brought chairs for us to sit and talk. The generator was running, so we could have light. I sat down and stared at both of them. They did not look like voodoo people to me. I had no idea what voodoo people looked like, but I didn't think they should look as perfect as this handsome young couple.

Paul William spoke in Creole, and Pastor Maxeau translated for me. The gorgeous lady was Lisa, Jeremy's daughter. She was also Samaika's mother and Bianca's sister. The gentleman was Lisa's boyfriend, and his name was Kenol. At this point in my life, I knew enough Creole to get a point across. However, my mind was so boggled by what I just heard, there was no way I could even put a sentence together. Thankfully, Pastor Maxeau could interpret for all of us, even though I am certain he probably filtered my conversation and made everything sound nicer than the way I intended. However, much of communication is non-verbal, so I knew they understood the absolute disgust and confusion that I expressed through my facial expressions, even if Pastor Maxeau did not tell them what I said, word for word.

As I was asking for everything to be explained, Bianca and Samaika came into the room where we were sitting and gave Lisa the traditional Haitian greeting of kisses on the cheek. Seeing this as confirmation of what I had previously heard, I glanced at Maxeau, who looked at me and nodded as if to say, "Yes, you understood the situation correctly." I waited for the kids to leave, and then spoke out loud as if I were solving a math problem. "So, YOU are Bianca's sister?" Lisa nodded yes. "And YOU are also Samaika's mother?" "Wi", she responded in Creole. I hung my head. I kept saying under my breath, "I don't understand." Then I looked up and said, "So that means that Bianca is Samaika's aunt?" Everyone in the room nodded their heads, yes. "So why in the world are those kids living in this orphanage?", I asked. Pastor Maxeau didn't even interpret my question for them to have an opportunity to respond. He just answered for them and said, "Because their elders can't take care of them."

"Why not?", I blurted out. "They look fine to me!" Again, Pastor Maxeau did his best to bring my anger down a notch or two, and then interpreted their responses. He said, "They both live with Lisa's mom." I tried to comprehend what this meant, and I said, "You live with your mom?" She said "Yes." Then I said, "And is that Bianca's mom also?" She understood that question and said, "Yes." Pastor Maxeau looked at me and said, "Calm down, Linda." I took a breath and then said, "I do not understand. If you and your boyfriend can live with your mother, why can't your daughter and sister live with you?" Pastor Maxeau seemed to interpret what I said. They both responded in unison, "Because there is no room, and there is no food. We do not have any money to send them to school."

I changed the subject and said, "Do you have any idea what has been happening to these girls?" They looked very confused. I began giving them graphic details of some of the worst nights I could remember us experiencing over the past two years. I told the stories at lightning bolt speed, and never once slowed down or paused long enough for Pastor Maxeau to interpret. He already knew all the stories, so he kept up with me, word for word. I think I passionately rattled off the details for a full two minutes, without taking a breath. Then, as I described Samaika beating her head up against the wall and floor for hours, I saw a tear roll down Lisa's face. It didn't even faze me. I kept going. I had two years' worth of stories, and I could go on all night long.

Lisa's boyfriend, Kenol, put his hands up in the air and interrupted. Maxeau interpreted, "Something must have gone wrong." "What?", I asked. "What do you mean something must have gone wrong?" Lisa responded, "When the girls were very young, they were both very sick. My father Jeremy did something to help them. It sounds like maybe something went wrong?" I yelled, "Ya think?" Pastor Maxeau did not interpret that. I sat on the edge of my chair, staring into the eyes of both of them. I asked, "What exactly do you mean, your father did something?" Lisa's one tear had now turned into many more. Kenol responded for her. "Paul William told us you know that Jeremy is a voodoo priest. Now you know he put a spell on the girls, so they would not be sick. Something has gone wrong with that spell, and we need to fix it." "We?", I asked Kenol. Kenol put his head down while he explained that he was one of Jeremy's assistants with the voodoo. He told me they could go and sacrifice a pig that night in a ceremony and it would resolve the whole situation.

At this point, I felt like I was in a movie scene and just didn't see the cameras. I responded back to Kenol, "YOU? You do voodoo?" He kept his head down and nodded his head, yes. He got up and started to walk toward the stairs to leave, and I said, "No! Wait! Stop!" He was standing by the stairs and said, "I know exactly what needs to happen, I can go now and have the problem solved by midnight." I could see Lisa out of the corner of my eye - still crying, but shaking her head yes in agreement, that Kenol and her father, Jeremy, could resolve the problems we had been suffering with for over two years in less than two hours.

I was so mad and frustrated and could not believe what I was hearing. I looked back at Lisa, and I asked her how she could be so sure this solution Kenol was describing would work. She hung her head and said, "I know because I am a voodoo princess." Oh my goodness, the children were right. The voodoo people *were* here! Pastor Maxeau just looked at me. I have no idea where the next words that came out of my mouth originated.

I said, "Kenol, Lisa…Do you know who Jesus Christ is?" Before I knew it, I was presenting the plan of salvation to these two voodoo people that I hated. The more I kept talking to them about Jesus and the plan He had for their lives, the less I hated them and by the time we were finished, I loved them. Both of them were crying by the end and stripping off voodoo items they had hidden under their clothes. They kept the items with them, at all times, for both protection and to use for spells and curses. They handed me red silk scarves, cross necklaces, and voodoo trinkets. As they took the items off and handed them to me, Paul William came and took them from me and burned every item in a fire just a few steps away from us. They both wanted to fully give and commit their lives to Jesus. Then Kenol stopped and said, "I need to wait until tomorrow to make my full commitment to Jesus because I need to go and help Jeremy sacrifice the pig tonight to release the spell on the girls." I yelled out, "NO! We are not going to do it that way. Today is the day of salvation! If you want to call Jeremy and have him do a silly spell, you can, but you are not doing voodoo spells anymore. Never again, from this moment forward."

With that, a huge smile of freedom came over both of their faces, and they bowed their heads and prayed their own prayers of repentance and asked God to forgive them. They renounced voodoo and asked God to help them with their faith and to make Jesus the Lord of their lives. When Lisa said "Amen" and raised her head, she looked at me and said, "I have so much more voodoo paraphernalia at my house. Can I please bring it here to you tomorrow?" I looked at Maxeau and he nodded yes. We agreed to meet back at the orphanage the next day. We hugged as if we had been friends for years.

**Do you want to know what happened with Kenol and Lisa the next day? Order your copy of *Choir of Angels: How 30 Orphans Changed Their World* today! To order, visit www.lovehimlovethem.org. **

Jeremy's Story (Part Two)

*Excerpted from Linda Gunter's *Choir of Angels: How 30 Orphans Changed Their World**

We drove through the busy Friday night traffic for almost two hours. When we finally pulled off the main road, there was no light to be found, not even the headlights from passing cars. It was very dark. I asked the driver to leave the headlights on so we could see where we were going to be walking. Even in the darkness, I could see that we had pulled into a place that looked like it used to be a very large home. However, much of the building was in ruins and there was no roof. The ground was covered in concrete and steps. I thought that we must be in a home that had been destroyed by the earthquake. As we were walking up to the house in the dark, Kenol called out Jeremy's name. Someone came walking toward us, but I couldn't see anything. We were out of the range of the truck's headlights. I am totally convinced that Haitians can see in the dark, but this white girl couldn't see anything! I was hanging on to the arm of my interpreter, Wilno, and following him with every step we took.

I heard some noises, and then someone struck a match and lit a candle. It resembled one of those short white candles that churches sometimes hand out at Christmas Eve services. However, this one didn't have that little white circular cuff to protect your hand from dripping wax. With the candle lit, I could see a lady carrying out several high back dining room chairs, setting them in a circle on the rocky, uneven concrete for us to sit down. Then, I saw a man with gray hair wearing a black bulky leather jacket and jeans. He was holding the candle. Lisa introduced me to her father, Jeremy. He had a very big smile on his face and handed me the candle. He told me to sit down. He reminded me of someone you might see sitting around a fire at a cabin in the woods. He looked much bigger than he really was because of the bulky, leather jacket he was wearing. The one thing he did not look like, however, was a voodoo priest. We all sat down in the chairs the lady had placed in a circle. As I moved the candle around, I could see empty liquor bottles laying around on the concrete floor. Jeremy looked at me and spoke to me in Creole, as if I understood everything he was saying. Wilno would interpret. Jeremy knew our meeting was a condition for me to proceed with the wedding for his daughter the next day. I started the conversation through the interpreter and apologized for not being at the orphanage earlier that day. I thanked him for going to the orphanage, and I thanked him for allowing us to come to his home. "Pa ge pwoblem, Pa ge pwoblem", he laughed, repeating himself several times, saying, "No problem." He continued, "What is it that you want from me? I am happy to do whatever you want me to do."

I noticed the candle dripping wax on my hand, but I couldn't feel it burning me. I just kept holding it up so Jeremy could see my face and I could see his. I told him I wanted to meet him because of the problems we were having in America with some of the choir children. He told me that Lisa and Kenol had informed him about the girls being sick. He said he was so sorry they were not feeling well. I told him his daughter was getting married tomorrow, and we really wanted him to come to the wedding. He said he would be happy to come. He smiled and laughed throughout the entire conversation. Then, I told him the main reason I wanted to meet him was that I wanted to introduce him to Jesus Christ. He called to a lady in another part of the house, and she brought him a Bible. He laughed and smiled and told me he knew Jesus. He started quoting scripture after scripture. The more he laughed, the more I started to smell alcohol. I finally realized the alcohol I was smelling was not from the empty bottles laying around, but it was rather from Jeremy. He said he knew I wanted him to do something with Jesus, and if I told him what I wanted him to do, he would do it. Then he started laughing even louder. I looked at Wilno, the interpreter, and said, "Jeremy is smashed, he's absolutely drunk!" Wilno agreed with me. I told Jeremy I really wanted him to come to his daughter's wedding the next day, and I would look forward to seeing him there. Knowing there was no possibility of a productive conversation, I was ready to leave. As I stood up to depart, Jeremy said, "No, wait, wait! You didn't tell me what you want me to do about God. What do you want me to do so my daughter can get married?" I said, "Nothing, Jeremy. I don't want you to do anything." He kept laughing. Lisa and Kenol looked very disappointed. They were apologizing for how drunk Jeremy was.

You could see the fear in their faces. They were scared that I might not be happy with the results of the meeting with Jeremy, and they feared I might call off the wedding. I handed the candle back to Jeremy and thanked him. I gave him a big hug and told him it was wonderful to meet him. He looked back at me and said, "You see, I am a very nice man, right? You see that? You see I love God, right?" I answered back and told him I was looking forward to seeing him at the wedding the next day. As we were leaving, the lady came back to retrieve all the chairs in the darkness. Jeremy quickly introduced the lady as his wife. I gave her a hug also and then held onto Wilno's arm for security and stability as we walked back to the truck. Lisa and Kenol took a tap-tap back to where they were staying, and I headed back to join the mission team at Pastor Maxeau's home. Tomorrow was a big day. We had a wedding to perform!

~

Pastor Maxeau and I left the orphanage and hopped in his truck. However, Wilno was not with us. I told Maxeau that I really didn't think I could find the place because it was so dark when we had gone before. I asked him if he knew where to go, and he replied with an unworried "No." A little confused, I asked, "How in the world are we going to find where we are going?" Pastor Maxeau did not even hesitate in saying, "Don't worry, Mommy Linda, the Holy Spirit will show us where to go." Less than fifteen minutes later, we were pulling into the dilapidated and broken-down cement building Jeremy called home. As we pulled in, Pastor Maxeau said, "Watch what I am going to do." He turned the truck around and backed in. Apparently having had experience with similar situations, he said, "When you come to these situations when the person may want to kill you before you leave, you make it easy so you can jump in the truck and leave quickly." I just laughed, shook my head and jumped out of the truck.

As we started to walk up the short hill through the broken landscape and pieces of cement, we saw Jeremy sitting on a small, preschool sized chair eating a plate of rice and beans. He looked up and saw me and immediately put his food down and came running toward me. He had on a purple voodoo outfit and what looked like powder all over his face. "Mommy Linda, how are you? Who is this with you?" I wasn't sure how to respond. He acted like we had been friends since the first grade. I introduced him to Pastor Maxeau. I think he had forgotten that he was completely dressed in his voodoo garb. There were several children there, along with their mothers. I learned later it was common to bring your children between Christmas Eve and New Year's Day to receive a Devil Shower, otherwise known as a Haitian good luck bath. That explained why the kids were there.

Jeremy had chairs brought over for us, and we sat down. I asked him why he didn't show up for his daughter's wedding the day before. He had no answer. I told him I was very disappointed in him, that he hadn't come. As I began telling him what a beautiful ceremony it was, I pulled out my phone to show the pictures. He kept looking at the pictures and saying how nice everything looked. And then I asked, "Do you realize because you weren't there for your daughter's wedding, my husband had to take your place to give your daughter away?" I showed him the picture of my husband walking his daughter down the steps. I was just about to continue scolding him for not being there, but I realized the moment he laid eyes on my husband taking his place, he completely broke down. To my surprise, he was actually crying. Before I could say the words, "You should have been there", he said, "I should have been there."

I paused for a moment to take in the grief on Jeremy's face. I said, "Jeremy, the reason I came back tonight was the same reason I came the other night. It has nothing to do with bribery, and it's not about the deal for me to pay for your daughter's wedding. You should know that by now because the wedding was yesterday. I already did what I promised. All I really wanted was the opportunity to present Jesus Christ to you. Well, and I curiously want to know why you are performing voodoo." Not fully understanding, he replied, "I told you I would do whatever you wanted me to the other night so my daughter could have a wedding." Again, I responded, "I don't want you to do anything because I want you to do it. I want you to change your life." I said, "Look around you. This place is horrible. Why in the world would you continue this way? I could understand if you were living in a beautiful house, or if you had nicer belongings, or any reason really. I don't see any reason you would do what you do, practicing voodoo. I can't figure it out". He looked at me and said, "Linda, I know Jesus. I know the Bible, but I can't surrender my life to him." Questioning, I asked, "WHY NOT?" All of this was being partially translated by Maxeau because my Creole was still a little shaky. Jeremy answered, "Because Voodoo is how I make my living. If I surrender my life to Jesus today, how will I eat tomorrow?"

When sharing the gospel in a third world country like Haiti, this question had become unsurprisingly common. "Will your god put food in my belly? Will he put a roof over my head?" My answer to Jeremy was the same as my answer to everyone else in Haiti. I replied, "Jeremy, you really don't think God can provide for you? God sent me here to tell you that He can provide. God can provide through me. If you could start any other business in the world tomorrow, what would it be?" He paused and thought and then responded, "I would be really good at selling liquor! I already have a great customer base for that, and many people will buy from me." I busted out laughing. "I don't think that would be an amazing business for you to be in. Let's talk about faith and how God does provide. Because if the only reason you are on Satan's team is because of how you think Satan is providing for you..."

Pastor Maxeau interrupted me and, in Creole, spoke directly with Jeremy for five minutes without pause. When the men finished speaking, and with a nod from Pastor Maxeau, I asked again if Jeremy was ready to give his life to Christ. I asked if he was ready to see what God could do. Jeremy took off the voodoo hat. He got out of his chair, dropped to his knees on the concrete, bowed his head and raised his hands to heaven. He prayed on his own, with neither Maxeau nor I leading him. He then began to strip off his clothing- ALL THE WAY DOWN TO HIS UNDERWEAR. He was singing and stripping off everything that clothed and adorned his body related to the voodoo. He was singing, crying, and praying. It was an unbelievable and glorious sight!

This is not the ending to this story that I would have ever imagined, but God had such different plans. Where I could only see evil, God had plans to turn it into good. God taught me an important lesson in that season about what it is to boast in the hope of the glory of God. Under my own power, Jeremy was as good as dead. Christ died for the ungodly, and that included the voodoo practicing, curse wielding, spell casting Jeremy. As we are reminded in Romans

6:8, "*But God demonstrates his own love for us in this: While we were still sinners, Christ died for us."*

Pictured: Linda stands with Jeremy before he accepts Jesus as his Lord and Savior.

Pictured: Look at the JOY on Jeremy's face after accepting Jesus as his Savior!

** Do you want to know where Jeremy is today in his walk with Jesus? Purchase your copy of *Choir of Angels: How 30 Orphans Changed Their World* today! To order, visit www.lovehimlovethem.org.**

The Ambulance Driver

Love Him Love Them has an amazing 24-hour prayer team. With all of the chaos, violence, and civil unrest affecting the country of Haiti on a daily basis, it is important to have a prayer team on standby for any and all prayer requests. Ephesians 6:12-13 says, *"For our struggle is not against flesh and blood, but against the rulers, against the authorities, against the powers of this dark world and against the spiritual forces of evil in the heavenly realms. Therefore put on the full armor of God, so that when the day of evil comes, you may be able to stand your ground, and after you have done everything, to stand."* With the armor of God and the power of prayer, the Love Him Love Them ministry is able to stand against all of Satan's schemes.

Shortly after plans were made to start the construction of Love Him Love Them's "Valley of Hope" hospital in Haiti, Pastor Maxeau told me he had found two ambulances available for purchase. My response to him was, "Pastor Maxeau, we haven't even broken ground for the hospital yet. Who buys ambulances without having a hospital?" Maxeau explained to me that we could not pass up the opportunity to buy the ambulances, and we needed to take a bold act of faith and purchase them. I heeded to Maxeau's advice, and we bought the ambulances.

In August of 2020, Love Him Love Them opened the Valley of Hope hospital in Haiti! After the grand opening, the two ambulances were used to transport those in need of medical care. During this time, violent gang activity had become quite prevalent throughout Haiti. Oftentimes, gang members would pull drivers out of vehicles and steal whatever cars were available to them. Towards the start of the gang activity, ambulances were spared. There were not many instances of ambulances being stolen by gangs. Therefore, our ambulances and drivers remained safe for quite some time. The ministry began using the ambulances to transport food and other supplies to our locations in Haiti. For a while, this form of transportation worked well in keeping our locations well-stocked with necessities. However, as violent gang activity continued to rise, driving the ambulances became more and more dangerous.

While driving an ambulance through Croix-des-Bouquets, one of Love Him Love Them's security guards, Eddie, was stopped along with five other cars and drivers by a gang. One by one, the gang members shot and killed the drivers of the other cars. Then, the gang threw the bodies into a ditch and stole the vehicles. The ambulance was stolen as well.

Needless to say, when I received news of this horrendous tragedy, I was incredibly disheartened. Of course, I was relieved to know Eddie's life was spared, but I was curious as to why he was let go by the gang.

I quickly learned that when one of the gang members pulled Eddie out of the ambulance, he made eye contact with him and realized he had been to school with Eddie at a young age. The two men were from the same area in Haiti and grew up together. When the gang member recognized him, he quickly pushed Eddie into the ditch and whispered, "Just play dead, Eddie." I cannot even begin to imagine the thoughts Eddie had in his mind during that traumatic moment.

Love Him Love Them's 24-hour prayer team prays fervently for the protection of our staff in Haiti. The Lord answered our prayers and protected Eddie, and he was not killed on that awful day. He is still here today, and he still does amazing work for the ministry. Our ambulance was stolen, but we are thankful to have had Eddie's life spared. For many of you, it may seem like I just told you a scene from a movie, but this is the reality Love Him Love Them faces on a daily basis. We have no choice but to trust in the Lord's protection over the ministry. Our battle is not with the gang members in Haiti. It is with evil forces and Satan. I encourage you to remember Eddie's story. Even in the midst of terrible circumstances, the Lord supernaturally shows up in miraculous ways to protect His children!

Pictured: The ambulance that was stolen by a gang in Haiti

Scan the QR code to hear Linda Gunter share this story on YouTube!

Chapter Six: Salvation

"For I am convinced that neither death nor life, neither angels nor demons, neither the present nor the future, nor any powers, neither height nor depth, nor anything else in all creation, will be able to separate us from the love of God that is in Christ Jesus our Lord." -Romans 8:38-39

I believe salvation is the ultimate miracle that Christ offers His children. Because of the sacrifice Jesus Christ made in His death on the cross, our sins are completely wiped away, and we have the opportunity to have eternal life with Him. As you read through these salvation stories, I encourage you to thank God for giving you the gift of salvation. If you know of someone in your life that has not accepted

Christ as the Lord of his or her life, I pray that these accounts will build your faith. Continue to pray for salvation over your loved ones. If you have not personally accepted Christ as your Savior, I want to ask you to refer to the end of the book, where a guided path to salvation is presented. What a miracle! We have access to everlasting life through Jesus!

Little Girl Speaks

During speaking engagements, I love to involve the audience in any way I can. Discussing things back and forth helps me to stay focused and engaged with the listeners. While I was speaking at a local church, I pointed out a young girl in the audience. I said to her, "You must be about seven years old. Am I right?" After I asked the question, the girl froze and became very scared. Her mom began to comfort her by giving her a hug. Although I was shocked by her reaction, I brushed it off as the child being timid and nervous in front of crowds. I continued my message, but I was a little concerned that I may have embarrassed the little girl.

After the service, I was doing book signings alongside some of the Haitian girls from Love Him Love Them's Haitian Orphan Children's

Choir. To my surprise, the little girl and her mother walked up to me at the table. As the mother was purchasing the *Choir of Angels* book, I decided to try a few things to help the young girl feel more comfortable. I kneeled down in front of her and said, "Hi! What's your name? I would love to personalize this book by writing your name down in it!" Again, the girl froze and backed away from me. I asked the Haitian girls to try playing with her, but she would not speak with them either. Then, the mother pulled me aside and said, "She doesn't speak." There was a very long line of people behind the mother, so I gave her my contact information and asked her to call me. I wanted to speak more with her about her daughter. Surprisingly, the mother called me a few hours after the service. I encouraged her to come by my house, and I asked her to bring her daughter as well. The woman quickly made plans to visit me with her daughter.

~

When the two arrived at my home, we sat down together. The mother began to explain to me that her daughter lost her speech during the COVID-19 pandemic. In addition to the loss of speech, the young girl was enduring a painful case of eczema and Graves' disease. My immediate thought after hearing the information from the mother was that this young child *must* have experienced some kind of trauma. It is well known amongst counselors and psychologists that loss of speech can occur after a traumatic event. It broke my heart to know a precious little girl could have endured such a difficult situation that would cause her to go from speaking freely to having absolutely no speech.

I wanted to pray over the mother and daughter, but before I did, I asked the mother, "Is your little girl a believer? Has she accepted Jesus into her heart?" The mom looked back at me and said, "I don't know. Isn't that something the church should take care of?" I explained to the mother that although the church can play a crucial part in building a firm foundation of faith through a Christ-centered community, it is important that parents raise their children in the ways they should go (Proverbs 22:6). Towards the end of our conversation, I presented the Gospel to the little girl. As I spoke with her about salvation, the girl gave me blank stares, and she did not receive the gift of salvation at that moment. Then, I proceeded to pray over the girl. I prayed for her eczema and Graves' disease. I asked the Lord to open up her mind and her mouth. After I prayed, I did not see immediate healing take place. However, I was confident the Lord would heal this little girl and bring her to salvation in His perfect timing.

A day after I spoke with the mother and daughter, I received a phone call. It was the mom, and she had very interesting news to tell me. That day, she had taken her daughter to Vacation Bible School. When she picked her little girl up, many of the VBS volunteers told her, "Your daughter wouldn't stop talking! She talked the entire time!" I was so happy to hear that the Lord opened the mouth of this precious child, and I was excited to share her story with my daughter, Jeanna. Ministering to children is one of Jeanna's God-given gifts. I knew that if I could connect Jeanna with the little girl, the Gospel could be reintroduced to her in a way she could understand best.

During the time of this account, Jeanna was in Greece for mission work. However, Jeanna made time in her schedule to video chat with the young girl. From all the way in Greece to Gumlog, Georgia, Jeanna led this little girl to Jesus. Within forty-eight hours, the girl's life was forever changed. Not only was she able to communicate freely again, but she gained eternal life with her Heavenly Father!

Who has God placed in your life to share the Gospel? *You* can be the instrument God uses to bring someone to salvation. I encourage you to walk in boldness! Satan wants to use the fear of rejection to hinder you from spreading the Gospel. Eternity is at stake for someone you know and love. Be confident in your faith to share the Gospel with those who desperately need to hear it!

Scan the QR code to hear Linda Gunter share this story on YouTube!
Episode Title: "Miracles with Mommy Linda-Little Girl Speaks"

Voodoo Request

One day, I received a very shocking message through my Instagram account. The message read, "Hey! I saw your contact on Instagram, and I was wondering, do you know a voodoo priest who could help me?" I almost found it humorous that someone would reach out to me of all people to request a voodoo priest! I decided to reach back out to the man who sent the message. I said, "Actually, I know someone much more powerful than a voodoo priest." The man asked me who I was talking about, but before I shared the good news of Jesus with him, I asked him where he was located. He said, "I am in New York. Can I still get some help?"

I proceeded to ask the man the specifics of what he needed assistance with. He explained to me that he had some health issues he needed help with. I couldn't help myself when I asked, "What about my Instagram page made you think that I could help you?" He told me that he thought he had seen me post something about voodoo on my social media account, and he figured he would reach out to me to assist him. I was unsure of what social media post he could be referring to, but I was determined to maintain a conversation with him. The guy admitted to being a twenty-three year old from America. I asked him if he practiced voodoo on a regular basis, and he told me he had not. Finally, I asked, "What is your specific health problem? Have you received a diagnosis from a doctor?" His answer to me was that he had a problem with his heart, and he experienced anxiety and panic attacks on a regular basis. The doctors he had seen told him that he could be experiencing a number of different things, but he never received a proper treatment plan.

I had to bring our conversation to a stopping point because I was on my way to a speaking engagement at a church. I asked the man if he would be willing to meet with me through video chat later in the day. He agreed and asked me again, "Will you be able to help me?" I responded, "I have done it before, and I know I can do it again." It is important to mention that up to this point, the man had no idea that I was a Christian woman intending to share the Gospel with him. Needless to say, I was very excited for the upcoming video chat. His final message before I had to leave to speak was, "How long will it take to fix the problem with my heart? How long until the anxiety and panic attacks go away? Will you do a spell? Or will you do something else?" And my final response to him was, "It can be instantaneous, and I will do *something else.*" I sent him the link for the video chat we would have later in the day, and I went on my way to the church.

Some of you reading this will understand when I say that Satan loves to interfere with technology. I cannot tell you how many times sound systems messed up while I have been speaking at churches. Thank God for my loud mouth! When it was time to meet for the video chat, there were so many technical issues. We had to switch between several different video chat apps before we were finally able to speak. Satan did not want me to speak truth and life over this young man! Thankfully, everything worked out, and I was able to have a conversation with the man I had been talking with throughout the day.

As we talked, the man explained to me that in addition to his health problems, he had not been able to hold a job for three years. He had many hardships to face, and it was causing him a great deal of anxiety. After we talked through some challenges, I had the amazing privilege of presenting the Gospel to him. I explained that the answer to his problems could not be found in voodoo or any other worldly practice. The answer had to be Jesus! He immediately surrendered his life to the Lord and accepted Jesus Christ as his Lord and Savior!

After our conversation, I connected the man with one of Love Him Love Them's board members for the opportunity to be discipled and mentored. I mailed the young man a Bible and a *Choir of Angels* book, and four days later, he had a job! Additionally, he had not experienced any signs of anxiety or heart problems since he surrendered his life to the Lord! It was so encouraging to see a new believer on fire for Jesus. Praise God for salvation!

Scan the QR code to hear Linda Gunter share this story on YouTube!

Episode Title: "Miracles with Mommy Linda-Voodoo Request"

Eldo's Baptism

To read Eldo's origin story, please refer to Chapter Seven: Joy.

Eldo is one of the children from Love Him Love Them's Haitian Orphan Children's Choir. He has been residing in Dawsonville, Georgia with my dear friends, David and Lisa Allen. I received a phone call from David Allen, and he said, "Linda! Eldo is getting baptized this Sunday at church, and he would love to have you there!" As soon as I heard the news, I was a little confused. A few years prior, Eldo had been baptized during the choir tour in Edisto Island, South Carolina. It was definitely a moment to remember because he was baptized at the beach along with seventeen other Haitian choir members. Why would Eldo need to be baptized again?

David explained to me that there was a revival at their church and the pastor made it very clear that if someone was baptized before giving their life to the Lord, that person was not truly baptized, just wet. I told David, "Well, before Eldo and the others were baptized, I presented the Gospel and led the prayer of salvation. After we prayed, I asked the children to raise their hands if they accepted the prayer of salvation. Eldo was one of the eighteen children to raise their hands." In my mind, I really did believe Eldo had given his heart to Jesus all those years ago. However, David explained that Eldo did not fully believe he had made a salvation decision in Edisto Island. Now, as an adult, Eldo wanted to make the decision to accept Jesus Christ as the Lord of his life, and he wanted to make this decision public by getting baptized. Although I had a speaking engagement already booked for the Sunday of his baptism, I canceled the booking. Then, I rounded up as many of the choir members as I could to attend this special day for Eldo!

It was such a blessing to see Eldo get baptized. This precious young man from Cité Soleil, Haiti stood in front of me as a mighty man of God professing his faith to his friends, family, and church members. I had seen the challenges Eldo had walked through, and it brought my heart so much joy to see him thriving.

Is Jesus *truly* the Lord of your life? Did you raise your hand at church or a Christian conference because it was the trendy thing to do at the time? When you accepted the gift of salvation, did you truly make a commitment to surrender your wicked ways? Did you get baptized, or did you just get wet? I encourage you to search your heart to find out if you really have a personal relationship with Jesus Christ. Maybe you have accepted Jesus as the Lord of your life, but you haven't followed through the first step of obedience by getting baptized. Baptism is a sign of submission to the Father and His will for your life. God has amazing plans for Eldo and for you too!

(From left to right) Mirlanda, Linda, Eldo, Jeanna, Redaphca, and Belinda capture a picture together after Eldo's baptism.

Scan the QR code to hear Linda Gunter share
this story on YouTube!
Episode Title: "Miracles with Mommy
Linda-Eldo Got Baptized!"

The Pastor's Ex-Wife Shows Up!

I have the amazing opportunity to speak at a different church every Sunday morning. Every week, a different congregation has the chance to hear about the things the Lord is doing through Love Him Love Them. One Sunday, I had a speaking engagement at an adorable little country church. When I first walked in, there was a Sunday school group meeting being held in the sanctuary. I entered quietly and sat to the side until the meeting was over. As I was listening to the Sunday school message, I noticed a woman sitting near me with her arms crossed. To be honest, she looked very angry, and it did not seem like she wanted to be at church. She would look at her watch often and sigh heavily as if she were in a hurry to be somewhere. Of course, I was very curious as to why the lady was in such a grumpy mood, so I decided I would talk with her after Sunday school ended.

When the class ended, everyone began to go their separate ways in preparation for the upcoming church service, but the woman remained on the church pew looking very angry. I went up to her and said, "Hi! My name is Linda. Is today your first time at this church, or are you a frequent member?" She spat back at me, "I'm Joni, and it's my first time." I explained to her that it was also my first time attending the church, and I was very excited to be there. Then I asked, "What made you want to come to this specific church this morning?" Joni's response to my question took me by surprise. She said, "The pastor is my ex-husband." What in the world? Why is this woman attending the church that her ex-husband pastors? I definitely thought that to be a bit strange. I said to her, "Okay..why are you here?" With a lot of anger in her tone, she responded, "Because he's been begging me to come for the last six years!" I thought it was so interesting how Joni chose to come on the one Sunday out of the year I had to speak at this specific church.

Soon after our conversation, the pastor walked up. He saw me speaking with Joni, and he pulled me to the side. He said, "Hi, Linda! I see you have met Joni. Now that you have met her, I would like you to come and meet my wife." Oh my goodness! I truly felt like I was on the Jerry Springer show! I was just hoping there wouldn't be any drama between the wife and ex-wife during my time at the church. Feeling a bit awkward, I walked over to the pastor's wife to shake her hand. She introduced me to the children sitting with her, and we made small talk. After meeting her, I walked over to another pew to prepare my mind and heart for my upcoming message to the congregation.

Joni's eyes almost popped out of her head when she saw me walking to the stage as the pastor introduced me as the speaker for the morning! I was very excited to have the opportunity to share God's truth with her and the congregation. I felt confident in the message the Lord gave me to share with the church members. After I spoke, I gave an invitation for people to come up to the altar for prayers of healing. The altar was filled quickly, and I joined the pastor of the church in praying over those in need of healing and miracles. After we prayed, I said, "If there is anyone here today that does not have a relationship with Jesus, I would love to speak with you and share the path to salvation with you." To my surprise, Joni rushed up to me at the altar. She told me, "I don't have a relationship with Jesus, and I have so many problems in my life." She began to explain the challenges she had been walking through to me. I went to find the anointing oil in my purse in an effort to anoint Joni, but I could not find my oil anywhere! I motioned to the pastor to come over so that I could ask him if he had any anointing oil I could use. When Joni saw me inviting the pastor over, she quickly stopped me. She said, "No no no! I don't want him to have any part in this!" I explained to her that I understood the pastor was her ex-husband. However, I was just trying to get some anointing oil.

The pastor brought over a little jar of oil to me, and he proceeded to pray over Joni. I could tell by Joni's body language that she was very uncomfortable, so I kindly asked the pastor to step away. Then, I sat down with Joni and asked her, "Out of all the things you mentioned to me, what is the main issue you want resolved today?" Joni said to me, "I want a relationship with Jesus. I don't have one, and I want one." Tears began to stream down my face. Six years?! The pastor had been trying to get Joni to come to church for six years, and the Sunday

I show up to speak is the same Sunday Joni decides to come! The Lord knew Joni had so much bitterness in her heart towards her ex-husband, and she wouldn't have listened to anything he preached. Therefore, the Lord sent *me*. What a miracle! Joni heard the plan of salvation through me, and she accepted! She completely surrendered her life to Jesus! Believe me when I say that the angry Joni I met before the service was a completely changed woman filled with the joy of the Lord!

Do you have a Joni in your life? Do you know someone that is filled with bitterness and anger? Are you the instrument the Lord will use to share the plan of salvation to the Joni in your life? I encourage you to share the goodness of Jesus Christ with those in desperate need of hearing the good news. *You* can be the miracle someone needs today!

Scan the QR code to hear Linda Gunter share this story on YouTube!

Episode Title: "I Thought I Would be on The Jerry Springer Show, but God had Other Plans"

Joel's Salvation Story

One Sunday morning, I had the wonderful opportunity to speak at Shady Grove Baptist Church in Cornelia, Georgia. I prayerfully considered what I would say to the congregation as I made my way up to the front of the church. As I was walking, I passed by a young man sitting in one of the pews. As I passed him, I heard the Holy Spirit whisper to me, "You need to speak with him." Of course, I had never met the man the Lord was urging me to speak to, so I was unsure of the reason why the Lord wanted me to speak with him.

I shared the Love Him Love Them story with the congregation at Shady Grove, but before I ended, I wanted to discuss the miracles and healings of the Holy Spirit. I was under the impression that the pastor of the church would speak after me, so I did not give an altar call to those in need of a miracle or supernatural healing. I made eye contact with the man in the pew again, and I pointed to him in front of the entire church and said, "Hey! What is your name?" He told me that his name was "Joel". Then, I said, "Joel, I'm not quite sure what it is, but I know something is going on with you. I would love to speak with you after the service." Shortly after this exchange with Joel, I finished my message and sat down on a pew.

After I spoke, the pastor stood up and said something that surprised me. He said, "There is no need for me to present the Word of God because the Word of God has already been presented through Linda. She has already given us a message that will challenge us and give us something to think about." Then, the pastor led the congregation in making a huge circle in the sanctuary. We all circled up and held hands, and the pastor asked me to pray to end the service. Before I prayed, I asked the church members, "Is there anything specific that any of you need prayer for?" One by one, members of the church shared prayer requests with me. One mother asked for prayers for her son, who was undergoing terrible allergic reactions. Another woman asked me to pray for a ten-month old baby named "Tate", who was in the ICU. Several others shared challenging circumstances, and we prayed over each request given.

After the service, Joel walked up to me. He said, "You wanted to talk with me after the service?" I said, "Yes! Of course! What is going on?" In a blunt tone that I wasn't really expecting, Joel said, "Well, I have no motivation to live or work. I am extremely depressed." I quickly empathized with Joel, and I wanted to speak truth into his life. I asked him if he came to Shady Grove on a regular basis. He responded, "No. I haven't been to church in three years." He went on to explain that it was a family member's birthday, and he was invited to come to church and have a birthday lunch with her after the service. Then, he told me, "Oh, and by the way, I have a son." I said to him, "Oh, so where is your wife?" Joel shared that he did not have a wife, and he lived separately from the mother of his child. However, they did share custody of the young boy.

Of course, as a parent myself, I wanted to know how Joel was providing for his son without having a job. I asked him why he stopped working and how he got in such a depressive state. He sadly responded, "My sister died two years ago. Since her death, I have been very unmotivated and depressed. She was murdered, and her killer has not been found, although my family knows who did it." After talking more with Joel about his story, I offered to pray with him, and he willingly accepted.

As I prayed over Joel, I asked the Lord to protect Joel's mind. I went to pray for the helmet of salvation over him, but I stopped myself. I said, "I can't pray for you to have the helmet of salvation because you aren't saved." Joel agreed with my statement and admitted that he had not accepted the gift of salvation. I told Joel that I had no problem praying for the things burdening him, but the bottom line was this: he desperately needed Jesus. Joel's response to me was, "What do I have to do?" I encouraged him to completely surrender his life to the Lord. I said, "You have an amazing story, and it can be shared to others as a testimony to what God has done in your life! Right now, you are telling your story of depression and grief through your wounds, but you need to tell your story of joy and victory through your scars!" With tears streaming down his face, Joel lowered his head and surrendered his life to Christ. Before he ended his prayer, he said, "Lord, I want to glorify you and make you proud."

After he prayed, Joel looked up at me. His tears of sadness had turned into tears of joy! The mother of his child happened to be in the church service as well. I invited her over and shared truth with her just as I did for Joel. My heart's desire is to see her, Joel, and their son become a family completely on fire for Jesus. Before I left, I challenged Joel to have a job lined up before the end of the week. I said, "If you do not have a job by Friday, call me. I will speak with my husband and have him hire you." I handed him an autographed copy of *Choir of Angels* with my phone number included. The light of Jesus Christ is radiating through Joel, and I am so excited to see the amazing plans Jesus has for him!

(From left to right) Joel poses for a picture with Linda and the mother of his child after surrendering his life to Christ!

Scan the QR code to hear Linda Gunter share this story on YouTube!

Chapter Seven:
Joy

"Come and see what the Lord has done, the amazing things he has done on the earth."
-Psalm 46:8

In reading this final chapter, I encourage you to reflect on all of the amazing things the Lord has done. Thank God for the miracles He has performed in your life, and thank Him for the miracles that have yet to come! We have a wonderful Heavenly Father who loves His children dearly. Miracles happen every day, all around us. There is so much joy in knowing we have a wonder- working God who cares for us!

Eldo is 21!

Eldo was a member of Love Him Love Them's Haitian Orphan Children's Choir, and he is from Cité Soleil, Haiti. If you are familiar with the country of Haiti, then you probably know that Cité Soleil is one of the most devastating cities in the entire country. Eldo had the opportunity to come to America with the choir, and he sang as a choir member for three years! Due to circumstances out of the ministry's control, Eldo had to return back to Haiti along with three other choir kids after the choir tour ended.

~

A man named "David Allen" had the opportunity to come on a mission trip with Love Him Love Them during the Christmas season. He worked alongside the mission team to pass out "Christmas Joy Bags" to the children in our orphanages in Haiti. These gallon- size ziplock bags were filled with toys, hygiene products, and other goodies for the children in the orphanages to open on Christmas Day! Towards the end of the mission trip, the team had a beach day with the four choir children who were sent back to Haiti, including Eldo. During the beach trip, David Allen and Eldo became best buddies! As we got back on the cage truck to drop the children back off at the orphanage, David sat right next to Eldo and put his arm around him. David made eye contact with me from across the bed of the truck, and he mouthed to me, "Does this little boy have a home?" Sadly, I shook my head no. At the time of this story, Eldo was seventeen years old, and I knew the likelihood of him finding a forever home in the United States was very slim.

When we returned back to the guest house where the mission team was staying, David called his wife, Lisa, who was back in the United States. He told her that he was planning to bring a seventeen- year- old boy from Haiti back with him to the States. Eldo had touched his heart, and he wanted to provide him with a proper home while he received his education. Lisa was more than willing to invite Eldo into their home! During their phone conversation, David's wife noticed a bracelet she had on her wrist. It was one of the bracelets Love Him Love Them's choir had created, and each bracelet had a choir member's name on it. She received this particular bracelet after attending one of the choir's concerts. After the performance, the children spread out amongst the congregation and prayed for those in need of prayer. Lisa remembered a sweet boy praying over her and giving her the bracelet to remember him by. When she recalled this encounter, she asked David, "What is the boy's name?" Tears began to stream down her face when David told her, "His name is Eldo." The bracelet on Lisa's wrist had Eldo's name engraved in it! Eldo was the precious boy that crawled over five other people in the church pew to get to Lisa to pray for her. She insisted that David bring this sweet child home.

Eldo is now twenty-one years old! He graduated high school in the United States, and he is still living with David and Lisa Allen today. He changed his last name to "Allen", and he is so happy to be a part of David and Lisa's family! This boy from Cité Soleil, Haiti is now going to technical school to become a mechanic for heavy equipment. Him celebrating his 21st birthday with his new family is nothing short of a miracle! We thank God for what He has done in the lives of David, Lisa, and Eldo Allen. I have no doubt that their lives will continue to be blessed!

Pictured: Eldo and David Allen during Love Him Love Them's Christmas mission trip

Pictured: A current photo of Eldo and David Allen

Scan the QR code to hear Linda Gunter share this story on YouTube!

Episode Title: "Miracles with Mommy Linda: Eldo is 21!"

**To read more about Eldo's story, I encourage you to read *Choir of Angels: How 30 Orphans Changed Their World*. To order a copy of the book, visit www.lovehimlovethem.org **

A Miraculous Mountain of Mashed Potatoes

In 2022, Love Him Love Them had the amazing opportunity to provide a Thanksgiving meal for 5,000 homeless, hopeless, and homebound individuals on Thanksgiving Day. The ministry has held this event for the last fifteen years, so we have become quite familiar with how much food is needed to feed a large number of people. However, this particular event was the first time we would ever serve 5,000! The most we had ever served before was 3,800, so we knew we had our work cut out for us!

In preparation for the Thanksgiving Day event, the entire Love Him Love Them team calculated every food item to a tee, down to tablespoons! We knew exactly how many servings of each food item we had available.

Individual servings of the turkey, green beans, mashed potatoes, cranberry sauce, stuffing, and desserts had been accounted for multiple times to avoid running out of food. It seriously felt like we counted servings 1,000 times!

The entire Kingdom of God came together to put on this Thanksgiving Day event for those in need. Local churches and businesses provided the food items and extra goodies (laundry detergent, blankets, clothes, Bibles, and groceries) for the 5,000 Love Him Love Them set out to serve. It was truly beautiful to see the community come together to serve. However, even as the food was beginning to be plated, I said to myself, "What if there isn't enough food?" I knew we had counted over and over again to ensure that we would have enough, but I was still very nervous to see how everything would pan out. Before I headed out with a group of volunteers to deliver meals to a women's prison, I rallied all the volunteers together to pray. During the prayer, we asked the Lord to multiply the food that was still being served. Our hope was that we would have just enough food to feed the 5,000 we planned to serve that day. Little did we know, God was about to surprise us all!

When I returned from serving meals at the prison, I had the opportunity to walk around and see how the event was unfolding. As I was watching volunteers serve on Thanksgiving Day, it brought my heart so much joy to know that 5,000 individuals across the state of Georgia would have the opportunity to hear the Gospel as their meals were delivered to them. As the serving line for plating meals began to slow down and come to an end, I began to realize that we had *extra* food. How in the world could this be? We calculated absolutely every food item, and there was not much room for any extra servings beyond 5,000. I could have taken a bath with all of the mashed potatoes we had remaining! I had to return several large cans of green beans to the grocery store because we never had to open them. My husband and I had to send full-size turkeys home with volunteers because there were so many left over. I was truly blown away!

Even in my shock, I was reminded of when Jesus fed the 5,000 in the Bible. Jesus had five loaves of bread and two fish, and He fed 5,000 men *plus* women and children. At the end of the day, there were baskets of food leftover! The same Jesus who performed the miracle of feeding the 5,000 fish and bread is the same Jesus who provided a wonderful meal to 5,000 Georgians on Thanksgiving Day! The entire Love Him Love Them team was thrilled to see how the Lord provided an abundance of food for those in need. I am so very thankful that the Lord provided wonderful volunteers and sponsors to help make this event such a success!

Pictured: Love Him Love Them's volunteers for the annual Thanksgiving Day event

Scan the QR code to hear Linda Gunter share this story on YouTube!

Episode Title: "We Calculated to the Tee and Then God Gave us More Than we Could Handle"

Do you want to know how Love Him Love Them's annual Thanksgiving Day event first started? You can find the full story in Linda Gunter's *Peanut Butter Crackers and Flip Flops*. To order, visit lovehimlovethem.org.

Belinda's Story

In 2010, the country of Haiti experienced a 7.0 magnitude earthquake that completely devastated the entire country. From the rubble, two children were pulled, leaving their deceased mother behind, and the two children were sent to the LifeSaver orphanage. The two children who were saved from the devastation were sisters, Belinda and Redaphca. Unfortunately, Belinda suffered a terrible broken leg, and her sister also had injuries. The two sisters were not alone in their suffering. Thousands of Haitians became injured after the earthquake, and about 220,000 were killed. It was truly a heartbreaking time for Haiti.

A year after the earthquake hit Haiti, I took a trip with my family to Haiti for the very first time. During our time there, we visited the orphanage Belinda and Redaphca were living in. I heard the two sisters sing along with twenty-eight other Haitian children, and at that moment, I knew I had to bring the children to the States for a choir tour. By the grace of God, the choir tour came to pass, and Belinda and Redaphca sang with the choir for three years in the United States! After the choir tour, Belinda's sister had the opportunity to stay in the States with a host family. However, Belinda did not have the same opportunity, and she had to return back to Haiti due to the lack of available host families.

During Redaphca's time in the States with her host family, I received a call from the host parents. They asked me what they had to do to get Redaphca's sister, Belinda, to the States to live with them. After seemingly endless paperwork, Belinda was approved to come to the States to live with her sister and new host family! Redaphca and Belinda both went on to graduate from high school as the Valedictorian and Salutatorian, respectively. I am so very proud of these two ladies, and I thank God for everything He has brought them through together!

~

The Georgia Haitian Chamber of Commerce selected three individuals throughout the entire state of Georgia to be recipients of a college scholarship. Belinda was one of the three recipients of this wonderful scholarship opportunity! After Belinda was acknowledged at the ceremony for the recipients, she was asked how she would use the scholarship money. Belinda stood in front of the crowd and shared about the devastating day in 2010 that took her mother. She told the story of how her leg was broken during the earthquake, and there was no medical help available in Haiti to treat her. Belinda shared that because of her experience in the earthquake, she wanted to use the scholarship money to go towards a college degree in physical therapy. Her heart's desire was to become a physical therapist with the sole purpose of helping those in need in the country of Haiti.

Belinda's life is a *miracle*! I pray that Belinda's story of overcoming the most difficult of circumstances will encourage you today. Trust in the Lord to pull you from the rubble of challenges and trials the world tries to throw at you. Thank you, Jesus for rescuing Belinda! It is truly a *joy* to know and love her, and I am confident the Lord will continue to use her in mighty ways!

(From left to right) Linda stands with Belinda and David Gunter at the Pwochen Lidé scholarship banquet.

Scan the QR code to hear Linda Gunter share this story on YouTube!
Episode Title: "Miracles with Mommy Linda-Belinda"

A Wrinkled Napkin and a Determined Heart

Galette Chambon is one of Love Him Love Them's locations in Haiti, and it is the home to a school and church under the ministry. One day, a pregnant Haitian woman came from the mountains of Haiti to Galette Chambon having intense labor pains. She arrived on a tap-tap vehicle, and it was clear she had a long drive from the top of the mountain to our valley location. The woman and her tap-tap driver stopped at our Galette Chambon location because they saw the school and church and assumed there was a hospital available in this seemingly well-populated area. In desperate need of medical care for the woman, the driver walked her to the school. The teachers tried their very best to assist the woman, but they did not have the medical training needed to deliver a baby. Sadly, the Haitian woman and her baby died during delivery that day. It was truly a devastating loss.

~

Pastor Maxeau is Love Him Love Them's "Man on the Ground" in Haiti. All of the ministry's affairs are completed through him, and he helps support the children, teachers, pastors, and employees in our care. When Pastor Maxeau called me to share the news of the passing of the woman and baby, my heart was completely broken. I ended the phone call by telling Maxeau that Love Him Love Them needed to open a hospital to help serve the areas surrounding Galette Chambon.

Thankfully, I was able to meet with Maxeau the very next day to discuss the process of building a hospital. To my surprise, he pulled out a wrinkled napkin from his pocket that he had been holding on to for ten years! On the napkin was a scribbled blue-print of the valley. It showed the school and church we had grown to love, and next to those two buildings was the drawing of a hospital. Pastor Maxeau said, "Linda, My dream for the Valley of Hope (Galette Chambon) was to have a church, a school, and a *hospital*. I have never shared this information with anyone because I knew the Lord would send someone with the same dream, and he or she would help this dream become a reality." With tears filling my eyes, I smiled at Pastor Maxeau, and I agreed to partner with him in building a desperately needed hospital.

Of course, I had absolutely no qualifications in the medical field or construction. I had no business in making this near-impossible dream become a reality. However, I knew God could perform a miracle and help make Maxeau's dream come true. I did what I knew I could do best. For three years, I toured alongside the Haitian Orphan Children's Choir, and together we raised thousands of dollars to go towards the building of the new hospital in Haiti. Everything was starting to come together, and I was so excited to see what the Lord would do in and through Love Him Love Them's hospital in Haiti.

On August 29th of 2020, during the global COVID-19 pandemic, our beautiful Valley of Hope hospital opened! Hospitals around the world were shutting down due to lack of medical personnel and supplies, but Love Him Love Them's hospital was prepared to run smoothly and effectively to serve Haitians in need of medical care. Even with travel restrictions caused by the pandemic, the Lord made a way for me to attend the grand opening of the hospital. I was so very excited to see what the Lord had done!

On the very first day of the hospital opening, I turned to see a Haitian woman waddling in the front door of the hospital. Pastor Maxeau looked at me and said "Oh, Mommy Linda! We are going to have a baby today!" I have never given birth to a child. I have twelve children, and I did not birth any of them! Needless to say, I was a little nervous to see how a woman could give birth to a child in a third world country. Even in my nervousness, I sat with the woman and held her hand as she suffered through labor pains. She did not speak English, and I knew very little Haitian Creole. I just trusted in the Lord to be a comfort to the both of us at that moment.

As I held the Haitian woman's hand and sang hymns of praise to help distract her from the pain, she gave birth to a beautiful baby girl! As I saw the baby's face, the Lord reminded me of the precious woman and baby who lost their lives just six years prior. Even in the heartbreak of their passing, the Lord saw fit to build a hospital. Now a mother and baby would be able to receive proper health care, and many more individuals would come to receive much needed medical attention. The Valley of Hope hospital is still running smoothly today. Even in the midst of political and civil unrest in the country of Haiti, our medical staff remains firm in their faith and continues to provide medical care to the community. To God be the glory for the things He has done!

Pictured: The beginning stages of Love Him Love Them's "Valley of Hope" hospital in Haiti

(From left to right) A Haitian doctor and nurse stand alongside the mother and the baby born on the day of the Valley of Hope's grand opening with Linda.

Scan the QR code to hear Linda Gunter share this story on YouTube!

Episode Title: "A Wrinkled Napkin and A Determined Heart"

Path to Salvation

If you do not have a personal relationship with Jesus, I encourage you to refer to the book of Romans in the Bible. The book of Romans provides a clear explanation of how one can accept the gift of salvation. If you would like to make the decision to surrender your life to the Lord and accept Him as your Savior now, please follow the three steps below.

1. Admit you are a sinner.

"for all have sinned and fall short of the glory of God." -Romans 3:23

"For the wages of sin is death…"- Romans 6:23(a)

Everyone has sinned and fallen short of the glory of God. *Nothing* you have done can keep God from loving you! The wages of sin without Jesus has a cost, and that cost is death.

2. Believe that Jesus paid for your sin through His death on the cross.

"But God demonstrates his own love for us in this: While we were still sinners, Christ died for us." -Romans 5:8

".. But the gift of God is eternal life in Christ Jesus our Lord" -Romans 6:23(b)

God loves you so much, and He showed that love when He died on the cross to pay for your sins! Because of His death, you are offered the free gift of eternal life through Jesus Christ.

3. Confess that Jesus is Lord, and commit your life to Him.

"If you declare with your mouth, "Jesus is Lord," and believe in your heart that God raised him from the dead, you will be saved."
-Romans 10:9

After you have confessed that Jesus is the Lord of your life, I encourage you to fully surrender your life to Him. God has a wonderful plan for your life. Trust Him!

If you decided to make Jesus the Lord of your life today, I would love to hear your story! I encourage you to call me at (706)-599-7525.

Closing Statements

I pray these real life accounts of the miraculous and supernatural have built your faith. I hope you feel equipped through the power of the Holy Spirit to ask for miracles to unfold in your life. The world wants you to rely on counterfeit gospel, such as witchcraft, tarot readings, and New-Age elements. I encourage you to lean into God's supernatural power. Miracles occur because they are ordained by God to happen as a way to reveal Himself to us. Signs and wonders still happen today! *You* can be an instrument in the next miracle you witness. Be quick to obey the Holy Spirit's instructions. Trust in Him always, even when you do not fully understand Him. The Lord is eager to perform a miracle in and through you! In everything you do and say, always remember to Love Him and Love Them.

In Christ's Love,
Linda Gunter
Co-Founder and CEO of Love Him Love Them
(706)- 599-7525
linda@lovehimlovethem.org

Please feel free to call or email me if you have any questions or concerns.

Made in the USA
Columbia, SC
20 September 2023

23008950R00153